Catherine W
AN EXTRAORDINARY ORDINA ⊍MAN

CATHERINE WELLS
WITH THE ASSISTANCE OF ROY AND FRANCES HAY

Sports and Editorial Services Australia

Published by Sports and Editorial Services Australia,
85 Fairway Crescent, Teesdale, Victoria 3328, Australia

First published 2004

Edited and proofread by Frances Hay
Cover and book design by Roy Walshe
Printed by Antony Rowe Ltd (Eastbourne), 2 Whittle Drive,
Highfield Industrial Estate, Eastbourne, East Sussex, England, UK

National Library of Australia
Cataloguing-in-publication data

Wells, Catherine, 1914– .
    Catherine Wells: an extraordinary ordinary woman.

    ISBN 0 9751970 1 0.

    1. Wells, Catherine, 1914– . 2. Authors, Scottish—
    Biography. 3. Dingwall (Scotland)— Biography. I. Hay,
    Roy, 1940– . II. Hay, Frances, 1943– . III. Title.

    828.91

Title page: Wearing my koala t-shirt and a
borrowed Akubra at a barbecue on the banks
of the Moorabool River near Lethbridge,
Victoria, Australia, in 2002.

CONTENTS

Fantasy

In the evening rush of feet
Along a slushy snow-bound street
I saw a child, a little lad
Weary, his face was sad
Against the buttress of a wall
His cap in hand out stretched
Imploring! Mouthing! Asking aid
Did my eyes betray me
Or, did I see a ghost
Of a seventeenth-century poor boy?
Alone! And lost.

PREFACE

CATHERINE WELLS (née Ross) is an extraordinary woman. At the age of 86, with the help of Ross-shire Voluntary Action, she published her collected poems and short stories and raised over £1000 for various cancer charities by sales around her home in Dingwall, Ross-shire, in Scotland. Growing up in a ploughman's family during the First World War and in the 1920s, she attended a number of schools around the Black Isle and Easter Ross. She left school at fourteen, but even at that stage she was keen on writing and had a great imagination. For the next seventy years, work, marriage, the Second World War and a near fatal injury to her husband, raising a family, and maintaining a wide circle of friends and relatives occupied her fully. She continued to write for pleasure and primarily for herself but still published numerous letters to the press, poems and short stories in a variety of collections and anthologies. Finally, in her eighties, she responded to some prompting from her younger daughter to collect a lifetime's material together for a publication, and *Cathy's Collection for Cancer* was the result. Subsequently, an extended visit to Australia resulted in *Catherine Wells in the Footsteps of Burke and Wills: My Australian Adventures*, and though this did not appear as a separate publication, elements of it found their way into the local press to the delight of her readers. In 2003 her daughter and son-in-law persuaded her it was about time she told her own story with a view to launching the biography on her 90th birthday in June 2004.

For the next year, each fortnight or so, a letter would arrive at the home of her younger daughter, Frances, and son-in-law, Roy, in Teesdale, Victoria, Australia, with the latest instalment of her life story, written, as always, on scraps of paper and the backs of lists, calendars and envelopes in a fine, strong hand, more legible than that of either of the recipients. Questions were posed over the phone at weekends and invariably answered in the next missive. Photographs and more poems accompanied the letters.

This book is the result and, while it is above all a family story, it recalls, particularly in its earlier sections, a vanished way of life which we are in danger of forgetting. The story is largely told in Cathy Wells's own words, though Roy and Frances have added a few words of context and some sections, relating to her husband Jimmy Wells's wartime experiences, for example. These extended sections are distinguished by a change in font size. Her poems and stories and photographs, some of which have been published before, enliven the book and we recognise the continued assistance of Elma Blackall and Ross-shire Voluntary Action in scanning material and sending it to Australia for incorporation in the text. The book was edited by Cathy's younger daughter, Frances, who filled some gaps from her own memory but also added to and improved the flow of the story. While it was produced primarily for Cathy Wells's growing family and relatives, we hope that readers outside that circle will share some of our pleasure in this account of an extraordinary ordinary life.

Roy and Frances Hay
Teesdale, Victoria, Australia, March 2004

1

A ROSS-SHIRE CHILDHOOD

I WAS BORN ON 23 June 1914 at Kinkell on the Black Isle in Ross-shire, Scotland. My father, William Ross, was a ploughman from Cromarty, who had married Catherine Munro of Invergordon in 1899. My father's family were from Cromarty, while my mother's father, John Munro of Lossiemouth, came to Invergordon to work on the railway. He married Catherine McLennan.

Photograph by Robert McLeod in John R. Crossland (ed.), *Britain's Wonderland of Nature*, Collins, London, n.d., but before 1952, p. xi.

My parents had five children: Annie (b. 1900), Isabel (Belle: b. 1904), Elizabeth (Bess: b. 1907), Alexander (Alec: b. 1909) and me, the baby.

Farming life in those days meant regular movement at term time, as workers were hired and let go. Most of the flittings took place on 28 May, which was Term Day, and in April a day was set aside for Feeing Day, when all farm servants had a day off. They all trooped in to the nearest town, standing on the street, which was an indication that they were available for employment; that is, to be fee-ed.

A formal family photo, taken in 1918 in Urquhart's Studio, which was near Low's in the High Street, Dingwall. Mother must have saved the pennies for a long time to afford this! Standing from left to right: Bess, Annie, Belle, Alec; Seated: Mam, me and Dad. Compare this with the informal photo on p.27.

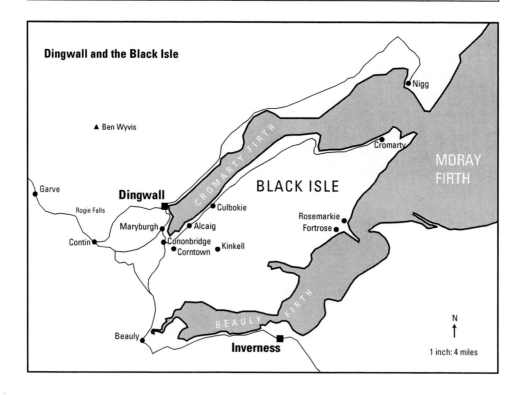

Dingwall and the Black Isle

Townspeople were always aware of this invasion, for the ploughmen were mostly pipe-smokers and the streets would be littered with spent matches.

Our family was nearly as nomadic as the tinkers and my father worked in various farms including Corntown, Badrain, Tighnahinch, Leanaig, Alcaig, Balavil, Humberston and Kinnahaird, where he died on 27 February 1940, not long after the start of the Second World War. My sister Bess once told me that we were twice in Corntown, but I don't remember that. I think the first time was before I was born.

Dad would flit at the drop of a hat for a shilling or two more or maybe a move up in the pecking order, not thinking that, from Mam's point of view, flitting was a dreadful upheaval. But Mam had this all down to a fine art. In fact, she used to tell us that some women never actually unpacked as they knew that next year at the May term they would be on the move again. We as children had to be decently, cleanly clad, that is fresh starched pinnies for the girls, on flitting day. It wouldn't do if the children were scruffy or the farm cart used for flitting was not scrubbed, especially if we had to pass some other farms. I always have a memory of Mam's precious geraniums perched on the back of the cart, swaying and wobbling precariously as we marched behind, long hair and ribbons to the fore. At least the Ross clan was as clean as Mam could make us.

Looking back on my childhood I revere the memory of my mother and many like her, who cheerfully bundled up all our possessions and moved to another cramped, inconvenient house, usually two rooms and a scullery, but minus running water and toilet, and began, all over again, to make a home. Scrubbing and disinfecting, papering, painting and making warm, they made a welcoming house, with a black-leaded grate winking in the firelight, a white pipe-clayed hearth and a fender which shone like silver with the help of emery cloth or the humble ash from the fire. The doorstep was also pristine white every day with pipe clay.

My mother's day started at five of the clock when she lit the fire and Dad went to the stable to feed and groom his pair of horses. My delight was to creep through from my own (shared) bed and climb into the kitchen bed in the recess, and in the soft glow of the lamp watch my mother make her daily baking of scones and oatcakes on the girdle aswing over the glowing coals. She used a whisk of hens' tail feathers to clear the flour between each round of scones and the oatcakes were set around a pottery jar on the toaster to dry off.

Girdle with oatcakes.

Nostalgia is a stealer of the truth, or putting it another way, nostalgia has rose-coloured spectacles. The summers, or any days of my childhood, seemed to have been long and halcyon days. I can only recall some winter's days, as all memories seemed hot and sunny. But, and I say but, the winter days were oh, so cold! Nothing in between, just two seasons. Summer and winter.

The harvest days were magic—the gold of the waving corn shimmers in my mind. The men cut long swathes all round the fields with the hand scythes, which needed a particular skill and a slow but sure method. Then came the reaper, horse-drawn, and the corn fell in abundance, to be taken up by the women who gathered up the stalks, wrapped the bundle with broad bands of corn stalks tied with a sure knot to make a sheaf, and stacked them in threes or fives, like old women leaning together telling a joke or some juicy scandal. It was arduous work and the followers of the binder had to keep up with the flow.

I wish I had had a camera then—it would have been a lasting memorial of these days. To take the afternoon tea to the harvest field was a ritual of pitchers with water and oatmeal, a true thirst quencher, and tea in huge teapots, with scones, butter oozing, and maybe wads of bread and jam. All stopped for a brief time, when the dogs went after rabbits—poor rabbits, but then it was a source of a good meal. Such is nature, dog eat dog, or rabbit. We were mostly all barefoot and developed a way of walking with a sideways motion, as the cut stalks of the now stubble were very sore on the feet.

Corn stooks.

Photograph by Donald McLeish in John R. Crossland (ed.), *Britain's Wonderland of Nature*, Collins, London, n.d., but before 1952, p. 109.

Then followed the other side of the coin. If it was a wet day the men workers had to turn the stooks. And Mam had to have clothing changes twice a day.

But also there was another rainy day occupation. When the corn was winnowed, it took place in the granary. I loved the granary—it seemed to have a lovely smell, maybe redolent of the sunshine of the cornfields. The men were quite pleased to be inside on a stormy day, but it was very dusty work. The corn was piled on the very clean granary floor and the machine, worked by hand, had fanners which separated the husks from the ears of corn. The dust flew everywhere and when we went with the half-yoking, tea and scones, you could hardly see the men in the thick haze. Then the corn was poured into sacks and it eventually arrived on our table as oatmeal from the miller.

I hated porridge then, but it has turned full circle now and I love it. But not in the true Scottish way, as I like sugar and the top of the milk. Dad had a ritual. He made brose with meal, boiling water and salt in a bowl. And beside it he had another bowl with cream. He used a horn spoon, dipping in the brose and then in the bowl of cream.

But accidents will happen and one harvest day Dad suffered a badly cut hand. The old-fashioned horse-drawn reaper had a rolling piece of canvas which conveyed the cut corn to a platform from which the stalks spewed out on the ground behind. The cogs and wheels

Measuring and bagging grain. A hand-driven winnowing machine in the background. The stoor has been reduced so this photograph could be taken.

Victorian and Edwardian Windmills and Watermills from Old Photographs, Batsford, London, 1977, photograph 106, from the Museum of English Rural Life collection.

underneath sometimes got clogged with stones and earth. One day Dad stopped the horse to clear under the reaper and the horse moved on, perhaps to munch a nice piece of grass. My father's hand got caught in the machinery. It was quite a gash so it needed stitches. The 'maister', Mr Tom Middleton of Corntown, had to take him in the gig into Dingwall to the doctor and in due course he came

Reaper.

The Illustrated Chambers Encyclopaedia, William & Robert Chambers, London, 1908, Volume 8, Peasant to Roumelia, p. 596.

Binder at work.

Photograph by Charles Reid in John R. Crossland (ed.), *Britain's Wonderland of Nature*, Collins, London, n.d., but before 1952, p. 110.

back swathed in bandages to join the women making the sheaves. No time off in these days. He always found something to do. As he seemed quite healthy, his hand soon healed and he was back on the job again.

Another job was tattie howking. We got a week's holiday from school (the 'tattie holidays') in October and the whole family turned out to lift the tatties. Children came from the towns in lorries to lend a hand. It was back-breaking work, but the money you earned would buy you a pair of boots, so it was worth it.

Ploughing matches in the autumn were always well attended. Competition was fierce in the harness class and the best matched pair of horses. My father was successful on many occasions, as horses and harnesses were his forte. Work for the competition started a month or two in advance. The best pieces of harness were collected from other horsemen, as the honour of their particular farm was at stake. Polishing went on every night with a 'beetle', a wooden tool shaped something like a dog's bone. My father had great faith in a compound of his own making. It was top secret, but I know it included beeswax for the final shine. The depth of polish on the harness was very important, as a judge would come along and bend collars or straps to see if the polish cracked. If it did, that was the end of hopes of success. My mother lent a hand making beautiful saddlecloths and

A plough team.

Photograph by Mondiale in John R. Crossland (ed.), *Britain's Wonderland of Nature*, Collins, London, n.d., but before 1952, p. 105.

lining the collars with red flannel. She washed and sorted out the flummery, a type of braid edged with bobbles in red, white and blue, which decorated the horses. Mam polished the brasses and the little silver bells suspended between the horses' ears, which made a musical chime as they walked.

To My Faither—a Plooman

Long ago and far away
There was an age, a Plooman's day
Tho' work was hard, he would agree
There was mirth and jollity.

Tho' day was spent in wracking toil
Wi' horses grimed an' weary
Yet the man was well content
His whistle sweet and cheery.

A hoosie snug against the cold
Firelight glow on irons bright
A wifie there wi' bairnies three
He thocht it aye a bonny sight.

His wants were few
His claes weel patched
But clean ye ken and neat
Tho' ill assorted an' niver matched.

A highlight was a plooing match
Where ferm rivalry was seen
Wi' horses decked in colours gay
And harness black agleam.

To win a prize they all did strive
With feerin' straight and endrig fair
Horses groomed and fetlocks washed
My! they made a bonny pair.

In thatching too he showed his skill
Stacks roped in diamond pattern
But alas! his day has passed away
A plooman's oot o' fashion.

Nae mair ye'll see on feeing day
On the street, in the toon
The bonnet-clad pipe-smoking man
That was the nation's plooing loon.

His way is past, who will regret
No one to tell his story
His love, and his care for his equine pair
Or his earthy couthy glory.

Ne'er day stocking.

Now, another tale. Christmas was not greatly celebrated then, but we hung up our stockings on Hogmanay and on New Year's Day we'd wake up to find them filled with sweeties, a book or a pencil, and an orange and an apple. Every time I smell orange peel it takes me back. I often call to mind that when I wanted anything which was out of reach my mother would say, 'Aye, ye get that when the cairts come wi' the money', and I believed her until I was quite big. I looked for this cart to coup the money in front of the door, as they did with the coal!

Millennium Memories

The scent of oranges brings to me
A whiff of Hogmanay when I was wee
In my stocking I would find
An orange in the toe.

I have lived a measure of this
So difficult to put in rhyme
All the wonder and the fears
All the laughter and the tears.

Cows that once were milked by hand
Horse and plough to till the land
Where once was sail, then came steam
Likewise iron gave way to steel.

Horse and carriage before the train
Then travelling by boat and plane
Lamps and lanterns, then electric light
And wasn't that a welcome sight.

Wars that showed the Nation's might
Men and women came forth to fight
Sometimes we had a glimpse of heaven
Then with grief our hearts were riven.

Kings and queens may come and go
Governments rise and fall, but this I know
That the stars are set in heaven and chariots swing low
But mankind's desire is to explore and colonise
Where'er they go.

And so
The race for space, the domination of the skies
All this I saw through an old woman's eyes
Computers now take the stage
The Internet, the wonder of the age
In taking over has the power
To change our world completely.

Convenient age! Even handy
To broadcast to all and sundry
That a new member has joined the clan
A little girl who can capture all our hearts
Will she travel all the light years?
Will she experience all the fears
The laughter and the fun?

So I'll end my tale as I begun
With the scent of oranges
And my memories.

Hogmanay was always celebrated in style and all the neighbours took part. It was a very, very poor household that could not manage a bottle of some kind of whisky. I remember my mother's ritual. All the house had a spring clean, sometimes newly papered, and at 11 o'clock or so Mam went into a frenzy. The fire was built up, the fireplace swept and tidied. We were supposed to be tidied too. A clean cloth on the table. The lamp glass polished, the wick trimmed to give a good light to welcome visitors, the floor brush handy. The bottle of whisky, shorty and plain and fruit cake, scones maybe, and six small tot glasses, as men, and I mean men only, drank whisky. Women and children had to do with port and blackcurrant and raspberry. On the stroke of 12 o'clock Mam opened the door wide and with the brush ushered the old year out the door and the new year in. Then Dad and Mam toasted each other and we as children got a wee glass of raspberry wine and a piece of cake. Then they waited for their first foot, a dark-haired man or a fair-haired woman. Mam and Dad liked to sing. One song was:

Man with a box.

Detail from the sleeve of Scottish Tradition 1, Bothy Ballads, Music from the North East, recorded by Hamish Henderson, School of Scottish Studies, University of Edinburgh, Tangent Records, London, n.d. Sleeve design by Robert Morgan.

'The fire was burning brightly, 'Twas a night to banish ... and all was singing old year out and the new year in' or 'A guid new year to ain and a', and mony may ye see, and during all the years to come, oh happy may ye be'.

After a few tots the dancing began. There always seemed to be somebody who played the box (accordion), a jew's harp or a moothie (mouth organ), and as the floors were usually plain wood and clippie rugs, they were quickly cleared. I remember one Hogmanay when we were in Balavil, one of the hired workers became quite stochious (I tried the dictionary but could not find the word, so I hope I have the spelling right) and was quickly carried away to the 'bothy'. On every farm there was a bothy and an orraman, an elderly bachelor, or a halflin, a young lad starting work, was housed in the bothy, which was usually a one-room annex to the main house. He did for himself and got a main meal in the kitchen of the big house. He usually paid one of the kitchen dames to give the bothy a redd out and to do his washing. Well, on this occasion he passed out at the jollifications and was put to bed. But the cantankerous person he was, he woke up ready to fight. He was roaring, 'Ye canna keep a rabbit in his hole', and he punched all the glass out of the window. But he hadn't the strength and was soon subdued. His name was Jock Roberts and he was always called 'Jock the rabbit' after that.

It was a simple life. But always had surprises.

Hallowe'en was pure joy. A nice turnip was hollowed out—a few hours' work— and a turnip lantern with a candle inside was made. All dressed up in the weirdest clothes, children and grown-ups sallied forth. Among the mischief that night, gates were taken off their hinges and left lying in the fields, chimneys stuffed with duffets, carts pushed out to the strangest places including the farm pond—and there was not a sign of any ill will. It was the spirit of Hallowe'en.

Turnip lantern.

I mind one Hallowe'en when we were in Alcaig and we were all out in force and went to the big house. The maister lined us all up in the kitchen, demanded our party piece and threatened to unmask us all. I was terrified! One of the servants put her hand out behind me and gave me a walnut. I never saw one before and I kept it for ages, until at last I consented to have it opened up for eating. How naive we were!

A trip to the town was rare but we saw plenty of people. I remember the fishman called regularly. Mam bought herring very cheap. Kessocks were about twelve for a penny, so small, just gutted, cleaned and fried. Oh, they were good! She also bought salt cod which she put outside on what was called a hake, something like a toaster with spikes which hung on the wall and we had to look out for the gulls. Mam would cut off a piece and soak it in cold water before cooking it. The baker also called with a horse-drawn van which had a wide drawer at the back for the sweeter cakes—gingerbread iced and Albert pink iced, one halfpenny each, and that was, with a rare loaf, paid for more or less by barter with six eggs from our hens.

Then there was the packman who travelled the countryside selling his buttons, ribbons, and needles and thread. He carried his wares in two big wicker baskets hanging from a yoke across his shoulders.

I also remember the tinkers coming round. They sold the pegs they made and my mother always bought some. Indeed, nobody who called at our house left empty handed. There was always a twist of tea and a poke of sugar to spare. The travelling folk fascinated me, with their strong-featured weather-beaten faces, and I used to wonder what it was like to travel the roads all the time.

The Travelling Folk

Children of the mist, the woods, the willow
The sky for a roof, green moss for a pillow
Free as the air, kin to the hare
Knows the moorhen's nest of straw
From the sedge, at the water's edge
Where the trout leaps, the farmer's neeps
Where the dog violet grows
All this thou knows
Travelling the road that leads to nowhere
All your needs of your life in the pack on your back
And if you lack anything
Nature will provide
No need of a guide, the countryside is yours to roam
A withy tent for shelter
For a space your home
No need to hurry
Until the wanderlust calls again
When the ground is fresh after rain
And the dog roses smell sweet
The loch is a mist before heat
Then in a fairy ring you may linger
Gather mushrooms if you hunger
A camp fire in the evening, a circle round and complete
Lighting up dark faces
Fiddle music and dancing feet
Rabbit stew in the pot
Not caring a jot for tomorrow
For the God who looks after the travelling folk
Is in the sun, in the air, all around.

But the tinkers were not always grateful for what was given to them! My mother told me about an encounter she had with a tinker wifie one day. After Mam had given her a mashing of tea and a few scones, the wifie asked if she had some clothes for her. My mother burst out, 'That I haven't. Can ye no see I'm as full o' patches as yersel?' The wifie was not pleased, so, as she made off in high dudgeon, she muttered, 'Kiss my ****!' And the wee bairn wrapped in the shawl on her back piped up, 'Aye, an mines, tae'. Mam was dumbfounded but she had to laugh!

Gypsy Woman

Down the road she came
The bairn on her back
In a faded tartan shawl
That was all
A proud tilt to her head
An attitude that said
'I will not beg or bow
I need some food, but I'll have you know
That I lived centuries ago
In another life
In which I was a Queen
In a splendour you have never seen
Another time when all the best was mine.'
Into her hands I put some bread
And milk, so that the bairn was fed
My cat sat on the window sill
They stared, black eye to eye
As if they knew each other's kind
Theirs was an affinity of the mind
She touched my hand, hers slim and brown
Rings and bracelets gold
Her manner bold
Her words I'll not forget
'You're blessed with love if nothing else.'
She strode away, her hips aswing
I do declare I heard her sing
With the cat, I watched her disappear
Into the rain from whence she came.

Life was very primitive then. As a family 'we were only one step ahead of the tinkers', but my mother's good management and my father's skills with horses meant that we children were well looked after, though the wages were not what you would call great. As farm workers we always had a roof over our heads at least. But a man could be sacked at a moment's notice and would have to uproot his family and find somewhere else to work and live. People left debt here, there and everywhere. One woman we knew had all boys in the family. They did not require as much as girls, who needed dresses and things. One day she came to my mother, 'What will I give to my man tonight? I've nothing in the house.' 'Give him porridge,' my mother replied. 'No, I gave him porridge at midday. He'll kill me, if I don't give him something different.' Mam gave her some suet and

Hawkers and travelling folk were a common feature of rural life throughout Scotland and Europe.

Frank E. Huggett, *The Land Question and European Society since 1650*, Harcourt, Brace, Jovanovich and Thames & Hudson, London, 1975, p. 125, from an 18th century work by G. D. Heumann, *Der Göttingenische Ausruff* (Seller of ducklings).

half an onion and told her to make skirlie. But that woman became a lady when the sons grew up and still stayed at home, so that the family income was much augmented.

In spite of all the hardships, my family was a happy one. My mother had a gaiety of spirit and my father a fund of amusing stories. They were both openhearted and never lacked friends.

To my mind, Corntown was the nicest farm we ever lived in. The farmer, Thomas Middleton, was a gentleman farmer. He'd been to agricultural college but had independent means. He farmed because he liked the life, so Corntown was almost a model farm. It was quite a big one, too: a grieve, six pairs of horses, a cattleman, a shepherd and, of course an orraman or halflin, a young lad fed in the kitchen. It was mixed farming: they sowed oats, barley, hay, turnips and potatoes, and kept cattle, sheep, etc. I don't know how many acres there were. Before Mr Middleton got the car he drove a smart gig. The family had two daughters, Peggy and Lelia. Mrs Middleton tended to play the lady bountiful. She'd come round the cottar houses with books, toys and clothing of such good quality that if you wore them you were an oddity and stood out in the crowd! However, I think in the main they had good intentions.

The housing was as follows. Six houses together and three in the Low Street. The shepherd's by itself, also the grieve's house separate too. The horsemen and the cattleman in the six houses. A lovely old couple lived in the Low Street. He was the gardener, a dead spit of the one on the TV series 'Bill and Ben'. We used to visit, my sister Bess and I. I think she did a message to be rewarded with a ginger snap biscuit kept in one of two tins on the mantel with sloping lids like a desk. I loved them. I was fascinated. I wonder who got them when the old couple died.

Now, this is gruesome but it fascinated me. The old lady had an ear complaint and always had a piece of white cotton wool taped thereon. Sandy, the husband must have been getting on in years and he often fell in the garden. The maister retired him and gave him the hoosie rent free. But what his age really was I didn't know.

The houses faced inwards with the back to the road, and opposite the door, across a wide lane, was an outhouse and a hen run where most of the tenants kept

Ferm toun and smiddy. This one is from the Isle of Arran in the Firth of Clyde, but similar ones could be found all over Easter Ross.

Ayrshire Life, 8, July–August 1984, p. 9.

hens. One neighbour lived with his old mother. He used to sit on a stool inside the hen run meticulously breaking up odd pieces of china grit for the hens to encourage laying. He was a canny bloke and had the reputation of having a bit of brass which, according to rumour, was buried in the hen run.

Behind the houses was a strip of grass, a dyke (stone wall) and the main metal road where we used to play and, whether it was natural or by usage, there was a wide hollow which we sat around. The games we played were five stones on the back of the hand and the aim was to flip them over onto the other hand without dropping any. One the boys played was something like the quoits that the men played with a horseshoe as the middle marker. But the boys' method was as follows. They balanced a clasp knife point downwards on the tip of the middle finger and tried to aim at the ground nearest a piece of wood stuck in the ground as a marker. We also played rounders and skipping, hop scotch (or peevers) and with our dolls. Mine usually was a stocking with arms and body and face stuffed with rags.

But I loved cats and I was never without one to love. Farms are never short of cats and most families had one and kittens came along in due course. A married couple on the farm had a baby and we were taken in to see it. It had black hair, which was all you could see. I thought, and said, that it was Snooks, the couple's black cat! I was very young then, two or three, I think.

There were always tasks to do and going to the well for water was one. I really liked this, especially in good weather when the hayfields were abloom with poppies, cuckoo-flowers and meadow sweet. The path meandered to a deep, free-flowing stream which was dammed and cordoned off to form a deep well. You could see the bed through the clear water with pebbles and minnows swimming. With a skillet, pure clear water was scooped up to fill two zinc pails. A 'gurd' (I think the word was really 'guard' but through usage it became 'gurd') made carrying water easier. It was a square of thin slats of wood which you placed over the handles of the pails, and you stood inside and they really did balance the load. So even I at a young age could manage to carry the water home without spilling a drop.

Mam always said that during the day she herself spent much of her time carrying clean water in and throwing dirty water out. Even when I married in 1933 the water tap was outside and was communal to six houses, and it was only when we moved to 5 Mansfield in Dingwall in 1945 that we had an inside toilet and running (cold) water inside.

Now, some of these memories are from during the First World War, when the harvest homes were all more or less cancelled or in limbo so that there was no ceremonial cutting and carrying home of the last sheaf, the 'clyack', which was usually nailed on the wall, maybe in the barn.

There were one or two things that I hated, yes even feared, on the farm at Corntown. One was the 'middens' and the cesspool. I will draw a veil over the 'middens'. But the cesspool was something else again. I do not understand even yet what was the need of it or why it was there or where the residue came from—probably something to do with the byres, which were dug out, replaced with clean straw and chaff, and the pure fertiliser spread on the fields. My brother Alec often described it as 'throwing **** at the moon'. It was done by hand, with a graip, and he hated the job.

Now, the other item which was irksome was the profound respect we were told to give the 'Maister' and his retinue, the lady and her two daughters. If we did encounter them on the road we were supposed to bow. Well, one day when playing rounders, the ball disappeared into a field of corn, a forbidden area to children. I was nearest and I had no sooner climbed the iron gate when we heard the clop clop of the horse and gig and the maister. My playmates all scattered to the side of the road and lined up to give the customary bow, and there I was left in the cornfield. Of course, I had treaded warily and did not disturb the corn or leave open evidence, so I squatted down and hid until he was well on his way. Just imagine that happening today!

Now, labour was scarce on the farms during the war and after the war the wheels of legislation turned slowly and the men had to wait their turn to be discharged. In Corntown there were labourers with no house to stay in, so Mr

Middleton asked around the cottagers if any one could take them, and Mam, always ready to make a penny or two, did. They slept in the room, in the double bed and, as they were English, I often wondered since what they made of the primitive practices on the farm and Mam's cooking over the open fire—porridge and mince and tatties.

I remember a concert being held in the village hall, maybe to raise funds for the war, and my sister Bess was one of the artistes. She had to go to the hall at night, maybe once or twice. But once especially there was a rehearsal just before the actual concert. Well, it was very dark, no lighting in the country, so Alec my brother went with her. In those days boys wore a Norfolk jacket, collarless with a belt and buckle at the waist, and a gutta-percha collar which fitted over the jacket and tied at the front, something like the collars and cuffs that nurses wore in those days. They just had to be scrubbed clean and were, of course, very white. On the way Bess and Alec heard voices and footsteps that seemed like maybe two men, so they hid in a ditch. And Bess had her hands around Alec's collar so that they would not be seen. They stayed a while to make sure the men had gone by. Bess always said they were very frightened.

Between Corntown and Newton of Kinkell, where my niece Effie (née McIntosh) and her husband Ken Kellow live now, was a loch, a sanctuary for gulls, and we, the kids, went maybe on a Saturday to see if the gulls were nesting. It was called the Rocky Loch and all around the edge were mounds or tuffets and in between there was water.

I was not allowed very far out in case I fell in. But I had a long pole with a spoon tied to the end. There were dozens and dozens of nests with their clutch of brown speckled eggs. I was not so keen on gulls' eggs—the yolks were a deep orange and the whites pale blue—but Mam was always able to make use of them. Now ducks' eggs I wouldn't eat at all. I always thought they tasted as muddy as the ponds they, the ducks, delighted in. But they were great in sponges and they turned out a very good texture.

I don't remember much of Kinkell Castle. Maybe what I heard my parents say. But there was supposed to be a tunnel from Kinkell Castle under the Conon River to Brahan Castle. I did visit Kinkell Castle relatively recently when the grounds were open one Sunday. Ilba Grant and I went and I met the current owner, Gerald Laing, a

Blackheaded gull landing on its nest.

Photograph by Mondiale in John R. Crossland (ed.), *Britain's Wonderland of Nature*, Collins, London, n.d., but before 1952, p. 177.

Kinkell Castle in 2000.

sculptor, who was interested to know that I was born there in the farm cottages. The four rugby players at Twickenham is probably his best known public work, but many of his statues can be seen in shopping centres. He is in the process of making a group of statues to commemorate the clearances in Sutherland, when the Duke of Sutherland cleared the land of crofters so that it could be taken over by sheep. More profitable, you see. There will be a man, a young boy and a woman with a babe in arms standing on a hilltop above Helmsdale in Sutherland, with the man looking out to sea and the woman staring wistfully back at what had been her home. It is ironic that this statue is to stand not far from one of the said laird, which is on Ben Bhraggie above Golspie. At one point the people of Sutherland wanted the statue of the laird removed, but in the end they decided on the new statue and a plaque to commemorate the past events.

Now, we must have moved from Kinkell to Balavil, a farm near Millbuie and more or less equidistant from Cononbridge. But I must confess I don't remember much about that—I was too young—except maybe what I was told about the time when our current puss was caught in a trap and Dad was at work not far off ploughing and came to the rescue. Wrapping his jacket tightly round the pussy's head, he managed to spring the trap and free the puss. Although it had a limp it recovered only to disappear up the chimney the day of our flitting! Nothing we did could coax it down and we had to leave without it.

When we moved to Alcaig, my sister Bess got work in the 'Big Hoose'. Cross was the farmer's name. I mind another funny story from when we were there. My sister Belle was a good singer and a bit of an actress, and one of our neighbours did not keep in good health. She had kidney trouble and on fine days she lay, well wrapped, on a settle at the gable end of the house. One day Belle tried to cheer her up by getting out the tin bath and putting a blanket and a cushion in it. Sitting in the bath, with a bottle in her hand, she sang this ditty:

> Goodbye booze for ever more,
> My boozing days are darn well o'er,
> Put a bottle of beer at my head and feet,
> And leave me there to die in peace.

Now, the sick girl nearly passed away laughing. But it did do her some good!

2

SCHOOLDAYS

BECAUSE MY FATHER MOVED from farm to farm frequently, my schooling was also peripatetic. I went to school in Cononbridge, Culbokie, Kinkell, Maryburgh and Contin. Bess, my sister, was at school with me for a brief time and Alec, my brother, for a little while longer. The leaving age was fourteen and Bess was seven years older than me and Alec five and a half. Annie, the eldest, was 14 years older than me so she left school about the time I was born, and Belle was 10 1/2 years older, so she, too, had left school before I started.

There was no school uniform—you wore whatever clothes you had available. The girls wore pinnies to keep their clothes clean and we wore button-up boots with segs (tackets) on the soles to prolong their life and went bare foot in summer. There were no school lunches either—we carried our own lunch, a piece and jam and often a flask of tea which was heated on the school stove. We had slates and slate pencils and always had a piece of damp rag or sponge to clean the slate. They were mostly one-teacher schools, and the classroom usually had a sliding dividing door, with the smaller or younger classes in one part and the older ones in the larger part. It was usually heated with a coal-burning stove.

I liked most subjects, but one in particular I remember well. We formed in a half circle round the teacher where she gave us mental arithmetic. I think I must have been quite a good student as I always had some prize at the end of term—money or a Bible or other book. The strap was certainly used, but rarely, at least on the girls, and I seldom got it.

I wrote this poem when I heard that many of the small country schools were to be closed.

The Little Schools of Ross-shire

The little shools of Ross-shire
Are aye sae dear tae me
Ritual pools of learning
Gems of memory.

Tae hear that they are closing
Makes me sad.

I remember when I went to school
In the summer in its glory
Aye, an' in the winter when it was cauld
Sna', frost an' hoary
Nae bus, just feet an' buits
Nae sae guid.

A flask o' tin wi' strong tea in
Set on the classroom stove
A cloakroom cauld tae hing yer coat
Dripping an' depressing.

But still the childish voices
Went soaring up tae the hymn o' blessing
Maisters kind and maisters strict
According tae their temper.

The leather tawse was aye there
Nae sympathy if ye whimper.

The tables all were learnt by rote
Nay fancy things, just facts
Were in oor minds weel packed.

At fourteen years ye had to go
Unless you had some sillar
Tae live an' eat an' earn a crust
A job o' sorts wis a must.

Into the university o' the world ye went
Wi' naething but yer good Scotch tongue
Nae Greek, like Burns to climb Parnassus
We couldna climb Ben Wyvis.

Still I ken it must be so
Wi' all the new inventions
O' computers an' the like
Canna be found for little schools
Scattered far an' wide.

Ye canna stem the tide o' progress
An' on that note I look back
I must be blessed
For very few are left of that dear past
That was my childhood time.

Ben Wyvis.

I first went to school in Cononbridge when my father worked at Corntown and I was there for about five years until we moved to Badrain, in the vicinity of Culbokie—another school, and some way to walk there, whatever the weather. But one episode I must record here about my time at Cononbridge School. We were never actually alone going or coming home from school and this day word somehow got through to us that there was a tribe of tinkers on the road ahead of us, and that they were a fighting lot and had been drinking meths, which could be had over the counter if you signed for it. I, like the younger ones, was very timid, and when we came across patches of blood, we all slowed up and really dawdled home. But we arrived safely. It seems that there was a fight and the police attended. The man and wife quarrelled and he struck her with a broken bottle with some injuries to her nose.

Before the school holidays it was the custom to be examined on biblical questions by one of the clergy of the churches. This particular year, in my last year at Cononbridge School, it was the Very Reverend Donald Munro of the Free Church. He was introduced by the headmistress and at the first question I put up my hand, as was the rule. He kept me standing and asked me question after question. The last one was, 'Who was raised from the dead?' It was the only one I hesitated on, but I settled on 'Lazarus', which was correct. I thought I might get a prize and I did, because Mr Tom McKenzie, the headmaster at Cononbridge, sent it on to Miss Fowler at Culbokie.

I still have the inscription page of the Bible I got as the Bible Prize at Culbokie School. My daughters Avril and Frances took the Bible to school and eventually it was in tatters, so I rescued the inscription page, which is now very much faded.

It is signed 'A. Fowler, Head Teacher' and it reads:

> *Culbokie P. School*
> *Session 1924–25*
> *1st prize*
> *Awarded to*
> *Catherine Ross*
> *Senior Division*
> *For excellence in Bible knowledge*

Now Culbokie School was very like Cononbridge School, which I was sorry to leave, as it was Term Day, 28 May, and the schools broke up some time in June for the annual holidays. I knew that I was due some prizes from Cononbridge, but now I would miss out because I had moved to Culbokie. Ah well, what could I do? In the end, Mr Tom Mackenzie, who was the headmaster in Cononbridge School, sent my class prize to Miss Fowler in Culbokie. My poly photos, which at that time were the official school photos, were also sent on free of charge, and I got the Bible Prize and a good report of my school work as well.

Church, the minister and the Bible figured prominently in our lives. When we were in Corntown we went to church and Sunday School on Sundays, but when we were on some other farms it was too far to walk to church. On Sundays nobody was allowed to play, knit, sew or do any of the ordinary weekly pursuits, though sometimes we would go for a walk with our parents on a Sunday afternoon.

As far as I remember the circumstances of our leaving Corntown were as follows. Mam was asked to foster two children for which she would in the future be paid. Now Mam was all for that, as it meant that she would not have to do outwork on the farm in all weathers. And as for bringing up children, that was what she had been doing for most of her life. But Dad, my Dad, was very proud and insisted on leaving our model farm to go to a remote place, Badrain, as he thought two more ragged children would not fit in at Corntown—and leave we did. So off we went, flowers in the tin bath, furniture in a farm cart, and to make matters worse it rained that day. It would, of course, and that night my lovely pussy cat, a tortoiseshell, was insisting on sleeping on my bed and Mam put her outside, and that was the last we ever saw of her. I cried!

Come daylight, things didn't look too bad in the new place. The hoosie was remote all right, smack in the middle of moor, whins and broom, and we discovered it was very boggy, as I knew later to my cost. Though it was nearer school and so we didn't have so far to walk in all weathers, I developed cold after cold as a result of getting rained on and having wet feet. Mam sent for the doctor. He had to come from Munlochy and God knows where we had to get any medicine if required. After a thorough sounding, the great man said, 'Och, she's thin. But you just keep giving her porridge', which I hated, although I do like it now. 'It's like a poultice on the tummy to keep out the cold', he said.

There was a stream alongside the house which I loved. Beautiful large king-cups grew in the marshy ground. Now Mam had these two toddlers to care for, three months old and one's birthday in January, Alex, and the boy, Billy, on 17 April. They brought their own love, although I could see them far enough at times. After school, this was the drill. 'Keep your eyes on Alex, give Billy his bottle … and so on'. Mam devised a great idea for playpens. She had two tea chests and in good weather when she was busy she dumped each one in a tea chest with something to play with. But the boy—man is ever inventive—rocked and rocked his chest until it fell over and then he upset the other one—the two rascals took some looking after, I can tell you! Billy, especially, was always into mischief.

The Beauly Firth and the Black Isle.

When the school holidays came I went to Cromarty to stay a few days with a cousin, Mary Gilmore, and was able to cross on the ferry boat run by the Watsons (for many years) on a Sunday School trip to Nigg, where the very notable rigs works are now. I got home from my holiday with a lift in a Foden lorry, which was something like the Australian long-distance trucks which have their exhausts pointing up into the air. My mother said I was like a little black girl, I was so dirty from the smoke, as I had to ride in the back of the lorry.

On the beach at Nigg, on the shores of the Cromarty Firth with the North Sutor in the background.

At Culbokie School I made two friends, one Cathma Bethune and her younger brother Algy, who always wore the kilt. Cathma was older, even older than I, but Algy was in the same class. Their mother, Maggie, and two older brothers lived in an attractive country cottage not far from the school, and they offered to take me home with them at lunch times, which I did most days and had many a good hot dinner. They were somehow related to Mr Bethune who owned the farm of Badrain, where Dad and my brother Alec worked. Either Cathma or Algy came up to the farm after four o'clock for their supply of milk. I was so very grateful for this, as in the winter it got so dark so soon.

Nothing ever stays the same for long, however, and we soon left Badrain and moved to Tighnahinch much nearer to Cononbridge. Belle, my sister, got married from there in May 1927.

Billy, of course, growing up, needed more supervision than ever. He was discovered one day in a field near the houses where the Clydesdale horses were put to grass. He didn't seem to be frightened of anything—he fell into a stream from the railing of the bridge thereon. How he escaped injury, I don't know. I don't remember Billy and Alex going to school. Heaven help the teachers!

Through the little village of Alcaig a leafy wild rose-bordered walk took one down to the sea shore, where there was a ferry to Dingwall. Once I remember going across with Mother when the firth was running high and I for one was glad to reach the Dingwall side of the ferry. The skipper of the Alcaig ferry was called 'Jumbo' and I remember on one crossing being asked to move around 'to spread the load'. To think that now you can cross the firth in the twinkling of an eye via the causeway!

The causeway from the Black Isle.

But to go back to my leafy lane which ended in a fair expanse of rocks and sand. It was ideal to play in and there was a deposit of blue clay which could be moulded into doll-size cups and saucers. Many happy hours were spent in that corner.

When my father moved to Tighnahinch I went to Kinkell School and it was there that I wrote my first story or rather essay. During the university vacations we were allotted various temporary teachers doing their practical in a country school. Two in particular I mind, one a Mr Patience who was red haired and prone to fitness, and often seen to frighten the natives by running the country roads in the dark in white shorts—he was short in temper, too! I once got five stripes of the strap, five on each side, for speaking in class. I was black and blue. Indeed, Dad and Mam were incensed and seriously considered making a protest, but they didn't. I think the teacher must have been crossed in love at one point, as he hated girls and preferred the boys.

Now the other was a complete opposite. He was one Alastair Frazer from Coigach, near Achiltibuie in the west, and he was a joy to learn with. One day he set us to write about anything that took our fancy and we were to submit it in a few days. And that was my first attempt at writing. Cutting it short, it was as follows. A little girl, who was in bed one time with 'flu and was gazing at the sunlight streaming in the window and lending a glow to the vivid red geraniums on the sill, was startled when a fluting clear voice demanded her attention … and so on. Anyway, the master was taken with the idea of the little fairy lighting up the dreary day of the bedfast little girl. He read it out in class, made it the focal point of a lesson, pointing out spelling mistakes and grammar howlers, and give it some praise, and I'm sure that, of itself, won me the class prize that year!

Soon it was the Qually exam, as our class was 12–13 years old, and a letter was sent to all parents saying that one or two of the best could attend Dingwall Academy. We were all about the same standard. My two friends, Daisy Grant and 'Toshy', Mary Macintosh, myself and one or two boys sat the exam. Mam and Dad told me I need not bother, as going to Dingwall Academy was out of the question. I would need a bicycle and a uniform, good shoes, gym clothes and money for a midday meal. But I did sit the exam and, as far as I know, passed. But that was that.

Then we moved to Leanaig near to where Toshy's parents lived at the crossroads. Her mother had a 'jenny a'thing' little shop there. I continued at Kinkell School, though.

After school, as I mentioned before, I had to carry the water for the house. In this latest house at Leanaig the water was available across the road, now a very busy one and altered very much from the days I talk of. There was a wheelhouse which housed the pump driven by a big wheel. We had to activate the wheel ourselves and it needed much effort, for me anyway, to fill the two pails and carry them across the road. Our hoosie was situated in what I thought was an ideal spot, with lovely views to Dingwall, and on passing that way in later years I have often thought that, if I had money, I would love a house there. Another dream!

Recently I was watching the news on the telly and it was highlighting the teenage gangs in the cities—girls all round a lamp-post carrying guns and weapons. It's a far cry from our long-past days in the country. We also congregated, but in those days somebody had a moothie or we played hide and seek.

When we lived in Leanaig, I still went to Kinkell School with Toshy, but as it was our last year, not much was really learned. Our coming home after school was as follows. We had a word with the 'stone breaker', who allowed us to grub around and find a really flat stone for peevers and some to drop into the, according to us, bottomless quarry further on. Depending on the time of year and weather, we called on an old lady (Kate), I think she was a sort of relation of Mary's, and got a bunch of daffodils or a bag of apples in winter time. I was so very glad to reach home, sit on the fender stool, eat Mam's delicious mince and tatties and read my school library book.

But the time passed so quickly and soon we moved to Humberston where the new Farmers' Market is today and then to Kinnahaird on the Contin/West Road where I eventually spent the last month or so in school.

I vaguely remember my sister Annie, and Belle after her, getting work in the house of the farm at which my father worked at the relevant time, then Annie went off to London when she was nineteen as an assistant, I think in the nursery, to some titled lady, whose name I am not sure of. Domestic service was about the only employment for females in the country and believe me they were grateful to avail themselves of it. It was very restricting work—you had half a day off a week and maybe every second Sunday. Sometimes you got a fairly good mistress and good food—but sometimes not. Everything was under lock and key. And, of course, you had to be back inside by 10 o'clock, which were 'elders hours'.

I remember hearing about this particular mistress who was fond of a tipple and when in her cups had a temper. One day something was not pleasing her, so, in a rage, she lifted the full bed chamber (the chanty) and flung it down the stair, narrowly missing the housemaid, who, of course, fled. She was lucky to have a home to go to—she would have been in dire straits if she had been an orphan!

I was destined to go into service but I had a family to go home to and, luckily, at the place I went to first, I was treated as one of their family.

An informal family photo, taken at Kinnahaird not long before I was married. Standing from left to right: Bess, Annie, Belle, Alec. Seated: Mam, me and Dad. I think here we must have deliberately been trying to echo the formal family photo that was taken when we were all a lot younger (see p.2).

My Granny's Shawl

My granny's shawl was left to me
I stroke it, soft lacy white
Lavender-scented, made to last
I know she knitted it just so
When she was in her prime
Click to and fro
As the cradle gently rocks
To fondly wrap around a babe.

Its first use a christening day
My mother said that it was she
That in its softness lay
Then in the family lent
Its purpose well fulfilled
Blessed to wrap around each babe
My granny's shawl was sent
When such a one was some weeks old
The shawl was used again
My mother did gently me enfold
To take my granny's name.

Time moves on and down the years
My parents are no more
I take the shawl and smooth the folds
A foundation for the future laid
I tuck around the lacy shawl
The shawl my granny made.

3

IN SERVICE

I LEFT SCHOOL IN 1928 at the age of fourteen and went to work as a general helper at Aultguish Inn on the road between Garve and Ullapool. I got the job through the grapevine. My mother was a member of the Women's Royal Institute and she heard about the vacancy from another member, Mrs Bethune, who ran the post office from her own home just as you entered of the village of Contin coming from Kinnahaird. Mrs Bethune's sister, Mrs Matheson, was the landlady of Aultguish Inn, which she ran with the help of her two nephews, Willie and Donald Tolmie. Willie was the elder and in charge of the bar and Donald was a general factotum, even roped in to do waiting at table and washing up. There was a cow and some sheep. To tell you the truth, I am not sure how many acres they had. There was a river that ran along the back of the inn and I'm sure there were trout in it. And they must have had fishing rights, as they regularly had a fisher for the season.

The housemaid.

So I was to go to Aultguish as a general dogsbody, though the work was mainly waiting at table and housework. I lived in and had full board and lodging. I cannot remember what the wage was, but I do remember Mrs Bethune taking me there with my little tin trunk. She drove a German car, an Opel, and her driving was … well, it was a good job that the roads weren't busy! When she came to a corner, she sounded the horn and shouted, 'Toot, toot, I'm coming', and God help anyone who stood in her way! But she was a darling. Years after I left, when

I was on my day off and at home on the island in Contin, I used to go up to the post office about 5 or 6 o'clock and maybe Jim would phone to say he was on his way. Mrs Bethune would say, 'Just stay for your tea, Cathy.' They had a little orchard with huge cooking apples and we would have apples baked in the oven with syrup and stuffed with raisins. They were very kind people.

Now, at Altguish I was treated as one of the family. Of all the places I worked in—inn, manse, doctor's—I would say the inn at Aultguish was the best. Many times during bad winter days we would not see anybody but the mail car which ran from Garve to Ullapool, as the inn was situated on the 'Jearie' and mostly snowed under—bleak and windswept.

Morning Mist

Day breaks 'neath the mountain high
Morning mist smokes the sky
River rushing, tumbling foam
Wide open, more freedom to roam
Silently behind a spur I stay
As the deer lightly pick their way
Down to the river, there to drink
And falter tensely on the brink
Now, as the mist is slowly fading
The leader stag, alert, is wading
Like soldiers, they string out wide
And, pass, like a mirage
To the other side
Did I see them? Or was it the mist
That formed the spotted fawns dew-kissed
Into fresh water their hooves clean rushing?
But lo! The sun breaks thru'
And up the hillside in full view
The noble beast, full antler spread
Proudly gathers up the herd.

But although the dwellings seemed few and far between people still got together on occasions. For instance, Willie Tolmie, the landlady's nephew, was engaged to the roadman's daughter who lived some miles away, and one night we were all invited to a ceilidh, which was super. There was a goodish crowd from all around. The *uisge beatha* was plentiful (not for me—I was simply not interested in whisky). But there was a blazing fire and lovely singing and, of course, plenty to eat. Another time we visited another croft down the road (as they said) 'just a bittie'. But it was a different occasion and there was only Kenny Morrison, a brother of the banker in the bank opposite Ian Morrison's father's bank in Beauly, and his wife and three children, the youngest an adorable baby. The croft was called Luibfern. I have since learned that this is a corruption of the Gaelic *Luib Feorna*, which means 'the bend where the alder tree grows'. Then again, once we all went to Garve, to a dance for some charity, and the folk of the glens turned out in full force. I met a Dingwall lad there, Jimmy Sheppard, a good bit older than I. But, as we were kent figures, he danced with me and in fact taught me a new step in the modern waltz, 'the wave'.

But time marches on and soon Mrs Matheson's new house was ready in Contin and it was time to move on. I had been at the inn for about a year and a half. But I'm going through my story.

Before I left Aultguish Mam did a credit deal with the blacksmith in Contin, who was then moving on to motor bikes, cycles and cars, and I got a new bike all my own—great! I paid Mam so much a week, as I, as a minor, could not get credit. So this bike was delivered to Mrs Matheson's new house ('The Faery Knowe') and it was kept there until I had time to get it. Eventually, on one of my days off, I visited the house and spent the afternoon with Mrs Matheson and her old mother. I think she was about 90 and they wrapped her in cotton wool. But she had good hands and made wool rugs, sea grass stools and basket-weave. She gave me a stool, a wicker basket and a small oval-shaped rug, which some years ago was used to wrap my cat, Tobee, in when we buried him in the garden at 15 Dewar Square. This was a parting gift and I was very sorry to leave them, but I knew that I would be welcome to visit any time. The old lady also made a complete stair carpet for the new house in colours of the heather. It was beautiful!

Just something else I remember before we leave Aultguish. The road was being repaired from Garve to the junction, a big undertaking in these days, with metal base and tarring. A huge tar boiler was used and the men were strangers, some Irish. Indeed, one I know of married a local beauty and his extended family still live hereabouts. One of the officials was an Irishman, Grainger. He stayed in Strathpeffer, but a lot of the men were billeted locally, so it benefited the inn, and, looking to the main chance, we had the surveyor and six workmen. The innkeeper had a lorry and employed a man and, of course, the bar did a roaring trade. The midday meal was sandwiches and thermoses, but there was a cookhouse and a bunk house built down near the river. Our six men and the surveyor had dinner at night in the dining room, though the surveyor had a table plus a cloth to himself. Whatever else was on the menu, venison had its place and there would be a huge tureen of mashed tatties, pudding, tea and scones etc. They brought a lot of money around. Come Saturdays, they didn't work and dispersed where they liked for the weekend, and one weekend Cookie was left on his own and got drunk and set the whole show on fire—cookhouse, bunkhouse and all. Dingwall Fire Brigade saved much of it, however, and it was soon built up again.

There was always plenty of venison for Mrs Mathieson's cooking—maybe a perk of the tenancy was to be allowed to take a stag off the hill. They had lots of old working tools, for instance branched candle moulds for the lard or fat, as every bit of the stag was used. I remember the cool of the dairy, with its flat

Aged 84, at Aultguish Inn in 1998, 70 years
after I began my first job there.

skimmers on a marble surface and shallow pans to hold the milk. There were
hand-turned churns and butter makers; the porridge was super with such creamy
milk. Port and plenty of it was used for cooking the venison. Of course, the bar
had all spirits at hand.

If there was class in Contin, there were no class distinctions. There was a
right community spirit in the village. Mam joined the Women's Rural Institute
(WRI). When there was a concert the village hall came into its own. We will take
a dance as an example. The band consisted of three instruments, piano, fiddle or
drums and accordion—'The Nippy Three'. And even if the music or the tempo left
a lot to be desired, we all knew the square dances so well that I think we could go
through the sets without the music—a set of tom toms would do; it was the beat
that mattered. When half past 9 or 10 o'clock came around, everything stopped.
The band stepped down and the clothes baskets with God's little helpers came
round and everyone got a cup of tea and then the eats followed—home baking
and sandwiches, which always tasted good. The WRI was in the kitchen and the
head of the team, Mrs Bartlett, the mother of Sandy Bartlett of local cycle racing
fame, my mother and all the other members did their bit. Then the band struck
up again, not finishing at 12 o'clock but at 1 or 2 in the morning. Exhaustion, but
a great time!

I just wish I could join in a good-going Strip the Willow or the Quadrille now! Everybody danced, no wallflowers there. But women on one side and men on the other and one big rush to get the chosen partner.

I really loved the Contin area—the church on an island with the Rev. A. C. MacLean, who married Jim and me in 1933. I thought of it as a magic place, something between Camelot and Brigadoon, and half expected the waters to sweep it all away.

Maelrubba's Isle

The Blackwater River makes its way
To Rogie Falls of lacy spray
Rushing, roaring, gushing forth
To split against a giant rock
And form an island.

Twin rivers now rushing by
Tor Achilty broods on high
Its bracken clad, ferny slopes
Like croziers in the hand of Popes
Look down upon the island
Maelrubba, Monk of Applecross
Extending his mission over Ross
In Contin created an Episcopacy
Or maybe a Catholic faith.

Now upon the island
There is a church, a manse, a glebe
A little house where once
We dwelt in happiness.

The beadle was the 'Minister's Man'
Who worked the glebe on weekdays
'Put the minister' in on Sundays
And was content
Upon the island.

Imagine it a fairy place
Maybe with an air of grace
A touch of mystery
Or of witchery
Who can tell?

The rivers encircled either side
In the sunshine seemed devoid of guile
But claimed the lives of children three
And in the churchyard you can see
The names on stone
On the island.

Where ancient monuments
To people now unknown
Lopsided and forlorn
Descendants are lying here
With kith and kin and siblings dear
Draws us back with memories dear
To the island.

Inside the church, one has to pause
To think upon what was, and is to come
To feel in the silence the presence of the deity
Relics of Bible, book and bell
Reference to ministers of yore
By the vestry door
A plaque to a former son
A friend to one, a famous poet
Who wrote words of lasting worth
An honour to our island.

The stained glass window rainbow bright
Sunlit colours, blinding light
Move lightly o'er the congregation
Standing to receive the benediction
On this our island.

Solemnly we take our leave
With many a backward glance
In case by chance
We see a modern Brigadoon
Or like the turquoise wings of a dragon fly
It will vanish on a speck of foam
On the rivers of our island.

Not so! The Church eternal will endure
For ages to come will be a lure
To take us back where silver strings
Bind us to the island.

The church dates from 666 and it was created by the Red Monk of Applecross. It was originally an Episcopal church with a thatched roof which went on fire, and then at some time it became a Church of Scotland church and manse. One window at certain times let in so much sunlight that it was nearly impossible to read or sing the hymns. But in later years a beautiful stained-glass window has been installed, beneficial to the congregation. Halfway down the interior was a fireplace then used to heat the church, but in later years this was discovered to be the crypt of some earlier saint and that is now inscribed thereon. There are also some ancient relics, for example a George III Bible where the s's are all f's and a bell on the wall. Near the vestry door is a plaque to one William Laidlaw of

Jamestown, Sir Walter Scott's amanuensis, his confidential secretary and a college friend, who is buried in Contin churchyard. Contin will always take me, draw me back. My father and mother are buried there and my brother and his wife, too, in the new churchyard.

Contin church.

With Jim on a shop staff outing in 1931.

4

Courtship, marriage and the Depression

IN DINGWALL, IN GRANT Street, there was a woman who ran an employment agency, something like the Job Centre today. I paid one shilling and my name was put on a register and I presume employers did something similar. I got one or two temporary jobs that way before I began work at a doctor's in Beauly as a house table maid. Now here's a coincidence: Bessa MacPherson, my friend, was leaving that very job I took over. The doctor kept dogs as pets and also racing greyhounds and he had a stud dog which was sent by rail with a tag round his neck. The station lorry delivered the dog to the house and I happened to be on hand to take delivery. He was a lovely dog—big, big, beside the racing ones. The doctor must have had independent means and entertained a lot. And the big dog simply would not stay in the paddock despite the six-foot high fences, and when I waited at table he padded around after me. They used to say, 'We only have the expense of Big Boy, as he clearly is Catherine's dog.' They lost one of the racers coursing over Culloden Moor. It fell over an unseen precipice. I was sorry. Another one was called Knightly Deed.

One day I was fed up as I knew nobody in Beauly, so I took my courage in my two hands and went to a dance in Kilmorack Hall. When I joined the bus which also took the band members, a very cheeky young man with his pals took the seat behind me. Amidst all the usual (man) youth talk, he put his feet up against the seat, nearly toppling me forward. I turned round and gave him the benefit of a furious stare. That was the first glimpse I had of Jim, who was to become my husband. I do think fate does have a hand in one's life. An inspector of the bus company whom I knew to speak to, much older than I, a lovely dancer known as 'Fred Astaire', gave me a modern waltz at the dance and he said that a young man in his company would like to dance with me and would he send him

The young lovers in Garve in 1932.

over. 'Well,' I said, 'it's a free country; just please himself.' Next dance Jim was there and from then for 54 years he was always in my life.

Oh, no, I tell a lie! I did see Jim once before that, but I did not know who he was at the time. One evening I was alone in the house where I worked. Cook was on her day off and the Mr and Mrs were out to dinner, so I was alone in the house. I didn't like it. I think I spent most of my life being afraid of something. I went upstairs to draw the curtains. It was raining cats and dogs. The house was on a main road and just opposite was a line of trees with houses behind that, and I saw this bloke sheltering under a tree on a bike. I wondered at this silly ass. I thought to myself, has he no home to go to. It wasn't until much later that I found out it was Jim. He had a date with a girl and she didn't turn up. Sensible lassie—I wouldn't have either, not on a night like that was!

Jim was 20 when I first met him. He was working in the licensed grocer's in Beauly and lodged at Cabrich. His father, John, was from Liverpool, but I cannot remember ever knowing where his mother, Elizabeth Brown, came from. They had five children: Jim (b. 14 December 1911 in South Everton, West Derbyshire), John (Jock), Lizzie, Martha and Jessie. His mother died giving birth to another daughter, Grace, who did not survive either.

Jim's father was a glassblower and the family moved to Glasgow for work. They were living in a sub-let (rooms in somebody else's house) and the tenant fell behind with the rent and they were all put out on the street. The welfare put the children into a home in Glasgow. It was common practice in those days for children from these homes to be fostered on crofts and farms in the North of Scotland, and Jim and Jock were fostered in the Black Isle, where, I suspect, they were often used as child labour outwith school hours. The girls of the family stayed in Glasgow and when Jim's father married again, they were returned to their father and his new wife. His father had a second family, but Jim never met his step-siblings.

Jim was not very good at keeping in touch with his family, though we visited Lizzie in Glasgow once when the children were small, and he attended his father's funeral in Glasgow.

Time went on and eventually I took Jim home to meet my parents and they liked him. He usually brought my father a whisky miniature, so perhaps that's why he liked him! I always told Jim that I stuck to him because he came to take me back on my day off, as I was (again) afraid to cycle alone on the dark nights.

We cycled everywhere—no car in those days. We were particularly fond of Rogie Falls and often took a run out there. Sometimes we took the bus to Inverness and went to the pictures.

At Rogie Falls in June 2003. No salmon leaping that day!

The Bonny Falls o' Rogie

The bonny Falls o' Rogie
Near the road to the west
A green woodland setting
Deep in a rocky cleft.

The countryside is beautiful
Where hills and lochs abide
There's Garve and Loch Achilty
And bonny Contin side.

Where the silent Black Water
By many a crag and pool
Flows on to make the Rogie Falls
In cascades foaming cool.

Orrin runs still and deep
From Fairburn down to Moy
Where we paddled at the water's edge
Full of childish joy.

But memory always takes me back
To the bonny Rogie sound
Where in its foaming waters
The noble fish abound.

There we roamed as sweethearts
And kissed in perfect love
The silver of the birch trees
The cloudless sky above.

Then cruel war showed its might
Duty called my love away
A vow we made on the swinging bridge
To meet on ilka summer's day.

A happy ending I now relate
After bitterness of years
With the sound of Rogie's rushing falls
Amid joyful happy tears.

Again we saw the rainbow
Then the silver flying spray
From a thousand sparkling jewels
To vapour on the air.

Blaeberries grew and heather too
Bog myrtle fragrant green
The willows trailed their silken skirts
In the rocky singing stream.

Now on mid-summer scents we come
On pilgrimage once more
To find the hills and lochs and falls
More lovely than before.

People change, the years pass on
But Rogie Falls remain
A lovely, dear and hallowed spot
To bring us back again.

Eventually we became engaged and were on the look out for somewhere to stay. But by this time the doctor's wife had had a baby. Now I had more work to do, a nursery to clean, and another fire to clean and tend, for which I had to haul pails of coal upstairs. In the afternoon I had to take the pram and two dogs on a lead for a walk. I just got fed up of this and put in my notice. They did not want me to go and offered more money. But I wanted to go.

Then disaster struck. Jim and his pal, Ian Fraser, were involved in an accident with their motorbike. They struck a bridge. Ian had cuts and bruises to his legs, but Jim had landed on his tail bone, the coccyx, and the doctor thought it might be broken. He was signed off work and, as labour was plentiful and jobs were so scarce, he was sacked at once. He came to live with us in Kinnahaird and for a time he had odd jobs on the farm.

But all was not lost. We heard there was a wee house for let in Adams Buildings off Hill Street; 38 Hill Street was the address. So we talked it over. We had £14–£15 saved between us and Jim was all for going to Glasgow to seek work. I would not go, so we decided to take a chance and get married.

With Jim, Ian Fraser and Barbara Morrison at Rosemarkie.

We were married in Mam and Dad's house on 29 December 1933 and, as the minister knew us so well (Dad was beadle of the church in Contin), he gave us a full church service with his minister robes etc. I was 19 and Jim was 22. Margaret McKenzie was my bridesmaid and Ian Fraser, Jim's pal, was Jim's bestman. I didn't have a wedding dress—we wore just our Sunday best—and no photographs were taken because we didn't have a camera and couldn't afford an official photographer. Mam made a lovely cold meat tea and somebody had a box melodeon and afterwards we went home to the wee house—no honeymoon! Neither of us had a job at the time, but Jim got unemployment benefit and extra for me as his wife, about 23 shillings a week.

We were lucky really, for we had our own door. Most couples at that time had to do with a room in somebody's house. I may say now that, for all the changes that happened afterwards, we were very happy there.

This was in the midst of the Depression, but through time, Jim got work, once for six weeks digging a drain for the gas works in Grant Street. It was work he was never used to (he was a grocer by trade), and the first wages were nearly all spent on a pair of working boots. Once we went back to stay with Mam and Dad, as Jim got a job at harvest time with a farmer. Sometimes I got a chance of holiday work and we made do, although it was a disaster if we broke the lamp glass, which cost one shilling and six pence. Jim smoked a packet of Woodbines a day. Five was about sixpence in the old money.

Then he started work with Henderson's, the ironmongers. It was through Bessa and Eck MacPherson that he got the job. Henderson's wanted some extra help in the agricultural store at the station during the busy farming season and Eck, who knew the boss, W. MacDonald, was offered the job. But Eck had three days at the mart and two on the dole and he didn't want to change the arrangement as it was regular, and this job was temporary. So he mentioned Jim's name and Jim got the job. Then the old man who helped in the store (Ilba Grant's grandfather) retired and Jim got his job. And so we had a regular wage coming in, maybe 30 to 35 shillings a week.

When I think back, economy was the watchword. Every penny was a prisoner!

Life always seemed to be high and lows, though. One day, six months after we were married, I took really ill. We had to send for the doctor, Dr Thompson. Doctors cost money, so you had to be really ill before you sent for one. I was admitted to the Ross Memorial Hospital, over the railway bridge. I didn't even know I was pregnant and the doctor said I hadn't enough blood in my body to sustain a baby. It wasn't poverty, just that the white cells were overtaking the red ones. They were so good to me and one night I was admitted to the theatre and

The proud parents with Avril Grace at the door of 38 Hill Street, 1938. We were so happy with our baby!

Dr Thompson, who was a surgeon, did the necessary operation. I was very ill for a week or more, and they told Jim to report every so often to the hospital as I might need a blood transfusion. I was in hospital for six or eight weeks. Well, to cut the story short, I was sent home to Mam and Dad with orders to eat milk, eggs, raw liver and raw steak. Well, the eggs and milk were plentiful, but I doubt if they could produce the steak! They finally got my blood up to 85 per cent and the doctor told me to get a dog or a cat, as I would not have a child for five years, so I got a cat, a black one called Tarzan.

Time moved on and eventually I was pregnant again. This time the pregnancy went well and Avril Grace was safely born on 12 April 1938 at home in 38 Hill Street. Her names were after the French word for the month of her birth (Avril) and Jim's sister who died at birth (Grace). It was a breech birth, so it was not easy, but Avril had all her fingers and toes and I survived, though, as before, I went about bent double for ages after it. But that too got better. Nature took its course.

Old Doctor Pender Smith was very much what I called a gentleman, in his sombre dark clothes, hat and grey gloves, which he slapped into his hat before handing it to whoever received him at the door. He implied that, if he had his way, he would arrange childbirth differently—a zip in the belly would be the answer!

In Inverness High Street in 1932.

5

WARTIME

THEN THE WAR WAS rumoured and Jim was called up. He was already in the Territorials, so he was among the earliest to get the call. He was enlisted into the 4th Battalion of the Seaforth Highlanders, which was part of the 51st Highland Division. To begin with he was stationed in the Ferintosh distillery buildings on the station side of Station Road in Dingwall, where they had just layers of straw to sleep on. Then he was put on a course at Catterick in Yorkshire to get his crossed flags as a signaller instructor.

The Seaforths at camp at Edzell. Jim is second from the left in the front row.

My mother and father at Kinnahaird in 1940.

During this time I was having nightmarish dreams, which seemed to me to actually become true later on. I dreamt of walking a long dim corridor and of being confined in a small space with others. Then I dreamt that I was near the church in Contin and I could hear singing and saw people in uniform. And then I dreamt of facing a mountain of coal and vainly trying to shovel it on my own into a tidy heap.

The first nightmare came true on 27 February 1940 when my father died in the Royal Infirmary, Inverness, and we walked along what seemed to be interminable hospital corridors, lit by dimmed blue lights as required by the blackout regulations, and all the family crowded about his bed. My father suffered for years with rheumatism and had kidney trouble. He was kicked by a horse some years before and, of course, the National Health Service was not really in existence then, so the injury was never really properly treated. My poor mother was distraught, and although we in our ignorance tried to comfort her saying, 'Mam, you have had a long happy life together', I will never forget her reply:

'Lassie,' she said, 'You don't know what you're talking about. The longer you live together, the longer you wish it to be.'

True. As many of us have learnt to our cost since.

The second nightmare was my father's funeral, which was held in Contin Church. My brother Alec and my sister, Bess's husband, 'Tosh', were both in uniform, and as we viewed the grave before the church service the next Sunday the Sunday School was singing.

My brother's wedding was fixed for a date in April that year, 17th I think, and Mam persuaded them to carry on, maybe in a lower key, as she was convinced my father would have wished it. So there we all were, in deep mourning with wedding favours to the fore. But such is life!

And the third nightmare was the worst of the lot. I later put it down to Dunkirk, the news of Jim's wounding, and the fall of France—but, again, I go through my story.

The Seaforths were moved to Salisbury Plain prior to going to France. Jim came home once, now a sergeant and, man-like, very proud of his stripes, and, indeed, he looked very handsome in his full uniform.

But then he had to report back to the regiment. I was terrified! What else was going to happen that dreadful year? I was so pleased to have my mother near at hand in 46 Hill Street, the house she had moved into after Dad died. The house they had lived in at Kinnahaird was tied to the job and when my brother married and was no longer working on the farm, it was needed for another worker and Mam had to move out. I was also pleased to have my sister, Bess, and her family in Dingwall, especially my twin nieces, Effie and Cathie McIntosh (as they were then), who often came to stay with me overnight. I was afraid of the dark, you see.

Financially, it was a difficult time, too. Our allowances and pay books didn't come through for about six weeks, but I had £2/10 saved for the rent and Avril, who was one year and five months old when war was declared, and I lived on that.

Sergeant Wells in full Seaforth rig in 1939 at their last camp before the war. He was taking part in a best-dressed soldier competition.

The period after the British Expeditionary Forces first moved to France was what was known as the 'Phoney War', and the 51st Division was stationed near Metz.

The 51st Highland Division's shoulder flash—as the troops called it, 'Hitler's Downfall'.

Jimmy Wells joined the Territorials, as the local battalion of the Seaforth Highlanders was known, during the Depression. As with many in his situation, it gave him something to do to overcome the boredom of unemployment. Signing up meant regular training including a camp, 'a free holiday under canvas', while the £5 bonus at the end was a tidy sum to supplement the family income. The Territorials were being prepared to supplement the regular army in the increasingly likely event of a European war. Each regular regiment was to have a Territorial equivalent. While in much of the rest of the country there was still a strong anti-war sentiment, in Scotland, and in the Highlands in particular, a strong military tradition was maintained. Jimmy's enlistment with the Territorials was due to expire in January 1939, but he decided to continue in the service.

When war was declared on 3 September 1939 the Territorials were called up and Jimmy was enlisted in the 4th Battalion of the Seaforths, which in turn was part of the 51st Highland Division, whose exploits in the First World War had already become the stuff of legends. Trained as a signaller, Jimmy was older than many of his colleagues and was quickly seen as leadership material, being made up to sergeant. The early months of war were spent working up on Salisbury Plain and then the regiment was sent to France as part of the British Expeditionary Force. The intention was that the Division would be stationed on the Belgian frontier ready to move forward in support of the Belgians, should Hitler decide to outflank the French defences to the south, as his predecessors had done in 1914. In fact the 51st was moved south to fight alongside French troops in the defence of the area between the Maginot Line, built as a line of strong points along the Franco-German border, and the German equivalent, the Siegfried Line, immortalised in the song which introduced the Dad's Army series on television many years later: 'We're going to hang out the washing on the Siegfried Line, if the Siegfried Line's still there'.

This was the period of the 'phoney war' when forces on both sides played cat and mouse along the frontier, testing each other's responses but not engaging in major operations. The British commanders were keen to have their troops exposed to battle conditions, as most of them, particularly the Territorials, had no experience of warfare and precious little training in combat. Unlike some French formations which had a very relaxed, live-and-let-live attitude towards the German front-line troops, the British units were encouraged to be aggressive and proactive. Stationed near Metz, the 4th Seaforths took part in this skirmishing, but then in May 1940 everything changed as the Germans began their typical blitzkrieg offensive with its right-flank shock troops pouring through Holland and Belgium, while heavy pressure was mounted on the Maginot line itself.

After a few days of fighting, it became clear to the Allies that the major decision would occur in the north and the 51st Division was assigned to bolster French resistance in the Pas de Calais. Getting there proved a logistical nightmare, as France's radial road and rail system was blocked by refugees streaming away from the invasion area. Some of the 51st went by train south of Paris, while other elements travelled by road in a variety of vehicles north of the capital. Cath says, 'I remember Jim saying that sometime when they were on the move he asked Lindsay, his immediate superior, what should he do with some of their equipment and he was told to throw it in the first loch they came to, and he did'.

Eventually the 51st was tasked to hold the line of the River Somme on the left of the French forces which were fighting a rearguard action in reality, though plans for major counter-attacks were mooted by the French

Commander-in-Chief, General Weygand. While the movement of the 51st was taking place, the British C-in-C, General Gort, assessed that it was impossible to stem the German tide and got the new Prime Minister, Winston Churchill, to agree to a British withdrawal through Dunkirk. So when the 51st took up its position along the Somme in early June, the bulk of the British army was being spirited away from under the noses of the German army and the Luftwaffe.

The advance formation of the German army had established a bridgehead across the Somme at Abbeville and the 51st was employed in a counter-attack to throw the Germans back across the river. The bulk of the forces engaged were French but General Fortune, commanding the 51st, was given overall control.

On 4 June 1940 the 4th Seaforths were given one of the toughest of assignments, to gain and hold the strategic Mont de Caubert. Advancing behind French tanks which were immediately disabled by mines or anti-tank fire, the Seaforths pressed on alone. In trying to cross over open ground they were subjected to withering fire, 'mown down like grass', according to Eric Linklater, and five officers were killed and 223 other ranks were casualties in this one attack, about half the battalion's effective fighting strength. The battle headquarters of the 4th Seaforths was also hit and the Commanding Officer, Lieutenant Colonel Harry Houldsworth, and two other officers were injured by shrapnel. It is quite possible that, as a signaller attached to Headquarters, Jimmy Wells received his wounds in this particular attack. He was 28 years old.

As he tells it, he was in a trench which received a direct hit and shrapnel struck him in the head. He lost an eye and was in imminent danger of losing his life. The remnants of the regiment were pulled back and the wounded who were capable of being saved were

The Seaforths' crest—Cuidich'n Righ.

transferred to the rear. For Jimmy Wells this must have been an appalling time as he was transported across northern France to the Atlantic coast and the port of St Nazaire, where he was taken off by the *Amsterdam* and brought ashore in Cardiff. In one sense, he was one of the lucky ones. His war was over and he had survived, though he was never the same man who had left for France only a few weeks before. Jimmy was mentioned in dispatches 'for devotion to duty in the face of the enemy'.

His surviving colleagues in the 51st, outflanked by General Erwin Rommel's Panzers, were driven back towards Le Harve, from where they were to be evacuated. Unwilling to move faster than his French allies who lacked motorised transport, General Fortune and the remnants of the 51st

Highland Division were forced to surrender at St Valery-en-Caux on 12 June 1940.

The 51st Highland Division was re-formed and fought with distinction in North Africa, Sicily and Northern France, finally being given the privilege of liberating St Valery after the D-Day landings. Many years later the Seaforths were given the freedom of Dingwall before they were amalgamated with the Camerons to form the Queen's Own Highlanders. Cath wrote the accompanying poem after that moving occasion.

St Valery

Do you remember St Valery?
If anyone should ask
The name of St Valery is written on the heart
And the ghosts of yesterday are marching
Marching down the street.

Can ye not hear them?
The steady tread of feet.

The kilts aswing, the ribbons flutter
That rest upon the cheek
The glamorous glengarries
That made our hearts to beat
Oh! How handsome they were
Those lads of yesterday
Who stirred the blood and caused the tears
As they marched away
With the pipes aplay, the drums abeat.

Can ye not hear them?
They're coming down the street.

Stand aside in homage
Bare your heads again
For the Seaforths are coming
Although 'twas all in vain
This is their last appearance
Before they vanish without trace
The tattered banners hang on high
In our ancient church
Our everlasting tribute
To those who suffered much
The medals given are so few
Though they needed no medals to be true
But they did receive an honour
Also given to the few
To march this street with bayonets fixed
And swords unsheathed
Eyes right saluting
Saluting them that's left
The men of St Valery
Truly were the best.

So stand aside, now let them pass
The unseen soldiers of the past
See! They've gone, the pipes are fading
The drum beat is silent now
They all have vanished
Vanished for evermore
Maybe forgotten heroes
But to us they will always be
The heroes of St Valery.

We will remember
How could we forget?
For the name of St Valery
Is written, written on our hearts.

Back home in Dingwall life had settled down and leave was started for the troops on active service and, indeed, some of the boys did get home. Jim was expected to follow suit, and Bessa MacPherson and I had started to paper the living room when a letter arrived from the 'No 4(?) General Hospital, BEF', dated 6 June 1940 and signed by an 'M. Rawlings for the matron', to say that 'Sgt Welles (sic), 4th Seaforths' had shrapnel wounds to his eye, hand and side, and was on the seriously ill list. This was closely followed by a telegram in a red envelope with a blue band marked priority, from the secretary of Whitchurch Emergency Hospital, Cardiff, saying, 'Regret James Wells dangerously ill. Should be visited.' The telegram said that if I wanted to visit him and could not afford the expense, a return railway warrant for two persons, one a relative, would be issued at the nearest police station on production of the telegram.

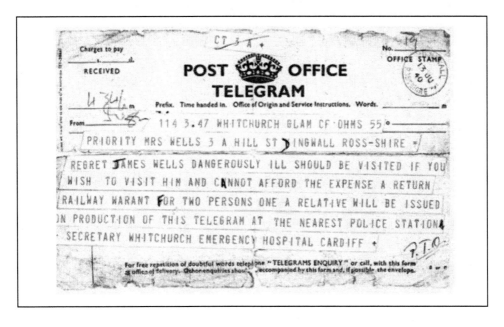

One item of interest I've learned recently is the identity of the telegram boy who delivered the telegram that fateful day. His name is Bobby MacDonald and he is married to Ella, a friend of my niece Cathie McDonald (née McIntosh). Though we have often met, that fact was never discussed. Strange!

The papering was abandoned! I think all Hill Street knew. There were actually seven lads from the area still in France and, of course, all their folks were agog to know what was happening.

I really didn't know what to do first. I had scarcely travelled further than the 21 miles to Inverness and here I had to go all the way to Cardiff in the blackout on trains crowded with troops of all descriptions! I was advised to have some one accompany me and Mam was the only one to be spared. My twin nieces came and took Avril home to their mother, my sister Bess. I was distraught at leaving her, but she did not understand what was going on and was very happy with the twins as they were often together. I could not wait until morning, so we got the night train.

Travel was severely restricted and there was a strict check at Inverness Station, lanes for army, navy and air force personnel, and then civilians. First change was Glasgow. We walked from Queen Street to the Central. A long haul to Carlisle and, I think, to Crewe, and then to a busy station, something like Didcot, near Oxford. I well remember the guard announcing the stations—Woolver-aampton! A long stop at Didcot, so we went for something to eat. So hungry we had salmon sandwiches out of a tin. I never liked salmon but was jolly glad to eat it that time.

When we arrived at Cardiff we had a wonderful reception by the Women's Voluntary Service. They were on duty at all stations. This was the first time I saw a car fuelled by gas; it was a taxi and it had a huge balloon on the roof. We were taken directly to the hospital. There we found Jimmy dirty, with a beard and a huge bandage covering half his head, but otherwise speechless to see us. We said … what did we say?—for the life of me I can't remember—vainly trying to connect, no doubt. But you cannot bridge the gap of time in a brief visit and we were weary, disoriented and finally taken away to where we were to spend the night in a lovely house, a solicitor's. Next day, after a sumptuous breakfast—no sign of shortage—we were taken back to the hospital and spent most of the day with Jim. He was given washing equipment and there was a lot of movement on the wards. A lad in uniform came along (I could not say what regiment he was in) and saying, 'Can I help you, Mac?', he washed and shaved Jim and took the basin away. Jim told me, much later, that he never saw him again. I had a brief word with the matron, who said that all these men were very fit and in good condition, which would help a lot with their recovery.

Arrangements were made for us to catch the night train going north if we could not stay longer, and so it seemed that in no time we were on our journey again. We were extremely glad to reach Dingwall. As on the journey south, the trains were overloaded with military personnel, lying, sitting anywhere, weary and spent, bewildered, lost their units and did not really know what was happening. I found Avril glad to see us but quite happy with Bess and the twins. Mam was out on her feet and, to tell you the truth, I wasn't in much better shape myself.

Then began the long separation of scrappy news etc. I was glad of my friends and Mam and my sister Bess and the twins. But Jim wrote of the kindness of the Welsh people. The boys in blue as they were called, regulation hospital wear, were allowed lots of perks, free travel, free entry to all entertainment, invitations en masse to houses eager to do their bit towards the war effort, and the factory girls adopted whole wards, sending paper, envelopes, stamps and many luxuries. In fact, Jim introduced Jock, his brother, to one of the girls, Joyce, when they were both visiting the hospital and later on they married. Jock is long dead now, but Joyce Wells is still in Wales and still in touch with me.

Jim began a long course of plastic surgery. A piece of bone was taken from his hip and embedded in his stomach to grow and live. He was in a ward with lots of men who were getting skin grafts. Some of them were airmen who had severe facial burns. They had 'handles' of flesh attached to their stomachs preparatory to being grafted on to their wounds, to make a nose, for example. They had to avoid knocking against these or doing anything strenuous. But some of the younger fliers, full of youthful spirits, were often in trouble with the nurses for having pillow fights and falling out of bed, so that they needed their handles stitched on again.

All nurses in the hospital were given a rank above sergeant because, as you very well know, the male of the species is forever chatting up any female and trying to get some perks not allowed. Now, Jim had a piece of bone grafted into the cavity where his eyebrow used to be, and when an operation like this was done, all bandaging had to remain in place, however dirty it got. The patient was sent out to another hospital for several weeks to free up a bed in the specialist hospital. During the time that Jim was in the other hospital, the bossy matron there insisted on changing the bandages. Jim could not prevent her doing this. If he had refused her ministrations, he would have been put on a charge, as the matron there had a higher rank—that operation was a failure. I believe the matron was severely reprimanded. Another piece of skin and hair was taken from the back of Jim's neck, which was deemed to be the most suitable to make an eyebrow. The only drawback was that the hair grew much longer than on his other eyebrow and it had to be trimmed frequently.

He got home about New Year time (1941), which was great, but alas he had to report for another year or so. I decided I would go to see him and we did, Avril and I. We were away for three months and Jim took us across to London, to Esher, to stay with my elder sister, Annie, her husband, Frank, and Freddy, their son. They were very tall men. Freddy had just enlisted in the Air Force. They thought Avril was the 'bees knees'—such a small person. After she went to bed at night, Freddy lined up her shoes beside his and in the morning he would tease her, 'Whose seven-league boots are these? Must be a giant around here.' They taught her to say 'Gor Blimey', and after we came home, all the kids in Hill Street liked to hear her say it with the London accent. Frank, my brother-in-law, was a lovely speaker, but his brother-in-law was real Cockney, born within the sight of Bow Bells, and he sounded it.

We tried to buy Avril a small tricycle which was for sale in Bentalls, in Kingston-on-Thames, but they were all spoken for and they would not take our money. But one of the cousins had a small bicycle and we took it home in the guard's van. I wonder where it went—can't remember now.

We were home again at Hogmanay (1941/42), the first time I wore trousers. We had an awful journey home. We were sided into a defunct line and they were bombing the train. And there were murmurs of complaint among the service personnel about civilians travelling, even though Jim was still in bandages. When Avril needed the toilet she had to be handed all down the corridor, so packed it was with everyone sitting or sleeping on their kitbags, only to find that the toilet had first to be emptied of three or four tired army/navy types.

Life sometimes had its lighter side, too. One day all the emergency organisations in Dingwall decided to have a combined exercise to test their response if we were invaded or bombed out. The kids loved it! My nieces were left lying at the top of the close against the wall. One had her legs all bandaged up and the other one's jaw was festooned in bandaging, with tickets tied on detailing their wounds. Along comes a doctor who was arranging their hospitalisation. 'And what has happened to you?' he said to the first one. 'My legs are cut and bruised and broken,' she said. 'And you?' he asked the next one. 'Oh,' she piped up, 'I have a broken jaw so I'm not supposed to speak.'

The adults and the younger children were all ferried up to the present Academy where the assembly hall was kitted out with cots, beds and bedding, lovely Navajo Indian blankets, and we were entertained and treated to a sumptuous tea until the all clear. I heard that all this was supplied by Lend Lease from America. I often wonder where it all went in the end.

Soon after Jim went back to hospital in 1942 he was discharged from the hospital and from the army. They could not do more plastic surgery at that stage. In all, he was in treatment for two years and eight months. He was angry at being discharged from the army. He liked the army and would have liked to stay during peacetime. And, though he had only one eye and therefore was not the best fighting soldier they could have had, he was a signalling instructor and his wounds did not detract from that. Mind you, I don't know how I would have coped with being an army wife. I was too timid for the moving around it would have entailed.

Jim gradually recovered from his injuries, but he was never the same man who left for war. Physically, he was never fully well again. His forehead sometimes ached and when he rubbed it his hand came away covered in tiny pieces of metal, like iron filings. His head was peppered with shrapnel, you see. He was changed psychologically, too. He remained a gentle man, honest and upright, and his brain was unaffected, but he now felt that he was disfigured and impaired. He had been a handsome man and had the confidence that engendered, but now he felt that people stared at him and that sapped his confidence. He just wanted to hide himself away. He was intelligent and, had he not been injured, I think he would have made something of himself, but after the war he seemed to regard each day as a bonus and was content to live his life quietly in the bosom of his family.

And I was so pleased to have him there!

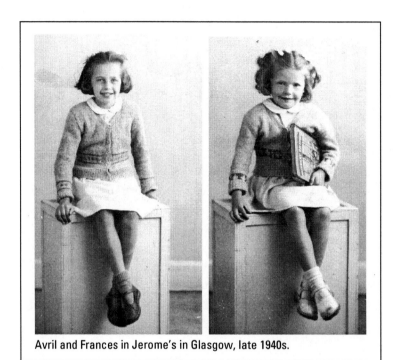

Avril and Frances in Jerome's in Glasgow, late 1940s.

6

Bringing up the bairns

GRADUALLY, LIFE SORT OF settled down and in 1942 I was pregnant again. During the pregnancy Jim was back in hospital for more skin grafts and when he returned I was in bed with the flu and the doctor was afraid I would abort. I had a bad cough. I recovered, however, and on 20 February 1943, Elizabeth Frances was born at home in Hill Street. We named her after Jim's mother (Elizabeth) and my sister Annie's (first) husband Frank, who had been so good to us when we visited them in London. We called her Frances.

There is a story attached to Frances's christening. The ceremony was due to take place on a Sunday at St Clements, but Jim received word the Thursday before to report to Edzell hospital for another grafting operation to his war wounds. The pulpit in St Clements at the time was taken by a Captain Dahl, a Norwegian padre, who was billeted in the Royal Hotel. It was arranged that he would do the ceremony privately in our own home, with just the padre, Jim, my mother, Avril, my twin nieces aged nine and myself present. There was a table with a white cloth on it, a Bible, a crystal bowl with spring water in it and a vase of flowers. It was so solemn, the only things missing being the congregation and choir.

Captain Dahl took Frances's birth certificate away with him and sent it back the next day, via his batman, with his signature and the official stamp of the Norwegian Army on the back, so that, he said, she would have a little bit of Norway in her life forever.

The Captain's parents were in occupied Norway and his wife had recently had a baby, which he dearly wished his parents to know. So one Sunday he preached a sermon and took for the text 'For unto us a child is born, unto us a son is given' from *Isaiah* 9: 6. One day he received a letter from his parents, which was heavily censored, to say that they were thinking about him and reading the

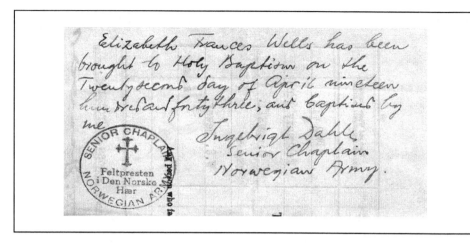

Elizabeth Frances Wells has been
brought to Holy Baptism on the
Twenty second day of April nineteen
hundred and forty three; and baptised by
me

Ingebrigt Dahl
Senior Chaplain
Norwegian Army.

Feltpresten
i Den Norske
Hær

Scriptures and glad that all was safe and well. He took this to mean that they somehow had heard about the new baby.

Jim returned to work at Henderson's and had an extra part-time job as barman with Ernie Sutherland in the Royal Hotel. We had no debts—if we could not afford something, we just did not have it. For 12 years we lived in Adam's Buildings and I can truthfully say that, although I might have more comforts as time went on, I was never happier anywhere else. It was a community where everybody was equal. Mass unemployment and shared war experiences made you humble, thankful for what you had.

Time moves on and where it went I have no idea. I expect we were too busy living. I mind the election when there were five candidates for the Ross and Cromarty seat—Malcolm MacDonald, Randolph Churchill, a Welsh doctor, and two others whose names I forget. I remember my twin nieces having red ribbons in their hair which were bought by their father, as he was Labour and so were we. Not that I knew much about politics: all we wanted was decent housing and decent wages and we would manage to cope.

We were getting concerned about how little room we had in the house

Modern-day Hill Street.

in Hill Street, now that we had another baby. We had our own front door, but only the living room downstairs, and one room upstairs with a sloping roof, in which we had one double and one single bed, a cot and a small wardrobe. A house belonging to Henderson's became vacant in Mansfield and I persuaded Jim to speak for it. He was too late, it was taken, but later another one, 5 Mansfield, became vacant and we got it. This was 1945.

I would have loved the first one, an end one with much more attractive features. However, we now had more room, and Avril and Frances had a bedroom to themselves. And we had tap water and a flush lavatory—it was bliss as far as that was concerned, though we didn't have hot water on tap. There was no electricity, of course, but we did have three gas jets for lighting in the kitchen, the sitting room and the stairs. I cooked on an open fire in the living room and we had fires for heating and, to supplement the gaslight, a big lamp, a small one, candles and torches—no tilly lamps; I hated their hissing!

Frances and Jim in Mansfield.

The gaslight annoyed Jim because it flickered on and off and he could not see properly, so when Jim got £20 gratuity money from the army we had electric light put in. Henderson's refunded the money later. In time I got a gas cooker.

But they never were right houses— they were built back to front and had no damp course, but we did spend many happy days there. Frances was two years old when we flitted and to begin with she regularly fell over the doorstep, as at Hill Street you walked right into the lobby.

Avril went to school the year we moved to Mansfield and Frances followed her five years later in 1948. They both went to Sunday School and to church with Jim and me, and eventually they both sang in the church choir. I remember Avi singing solo in church and at a concert in the Town Hall. They joined the Brownies and later the Guides. Avi became a rabid follower of Ross County and used to delight in twirling her rickety at the matches she went to with Jim. They went to dancing classes with Dorothy

Avril (or Avi as it was shortened to) and Frances in Urquhart's Studio in Dingwall in 1945.

Some of the Dorothy Gollan dancing troupe in the 1950s, probably taken at the Ben Wyvis Hotel preparatory to entertaining the tourists. Back row, left to right: Marie Macrae, Ethel Mackay, Avril, Hugh Chisholm; front row: Frances, Lloyd Gollan and Ann McIntosh, my sister Bess's youngest daughter.

Gollan and there were costumes and shoes to buy or make. I remember Jim tacking a piece of metal to the tips of the toes of a pair of red shoes and gouging out a hole in each heel in which he fixed two halfpennies so that they rattled, and that was the girls' tap dancing shoes. I and the other mothers made the costumes for the concerts the dancing troupe put on in the Town Hall—I particularly remember costumes for the gavotte, the cakewalk, a clog dance and a marching dance when they were dressed as soldiers and marched to 'There's something about a soldier …' and 'We're soldiers of the Queen …'. I wish I had a penny for the nights I worked on them into the wee small hours and for the number of times I watched them practise their dancing! The big expense, though, was the Highland Dress, with its dancing pumps, kilt and kilt pin, sporran, doublet, plaid and cairngorm, jabot, diced stockings and flashes, and bonnet with the blackcock feather and smaller cairngorm badge. Some of the items had to be bought. The pumps wore out quickly and, of course, the children's feet grew fast, so they needed to be renewed often. The kilts and doublets could be made, though I was not skilled enough to do them so I got Katie Grant to make them.

A Dingwall Lady

I know a little lady
Who is now of mature age
She did sewing for a living
But had a way of giving
One so often found in every town
Provides a place to sit you down
A room for you when newly wed
Lodging for a lad and also fed
So in passing you mention he or she
Oh yes, I remember him
He used to stay with me.

Making an acquaintance
Of someone newly met
Miss so and so would tell you
These two I'll not forget
The good times we had
When they were staying here
My, she was a sweet thing!
And him I'll aye hold dear.

Oh aye, they come an' see me
A card with Christmas rhyme
In fact, her mantelpiece
Is crowded all the time
With holiday postcards
From places near and far
The doorbell is always ringing
Some people with a car
To see Miss so and so
To take her for a drive
You know, you were on our mind
Just to see if you were alive.

And when talking of the sewing
Gowns for a bygone ball
I think I see them hanging
Like butterflies on the wall
There was so and so's wedding
My, that was a grand affair!
Yes, I made all the dresses
I was an honoured guest there
And kilts for the kiddies
Indeed, I can say
The many mums blessed her
When pennies were so rare.

Maybe her day is passing
But she was one of good intent
With cheerful witty sayings
And good advice, well meant
A store of pithy knowledge
Of folk of bygone time
A happy disposition
With a wide and beaming smile.

To visit was a pleasure
To listen was to gain
You leave her with her blessing
That draws you back again.

The children were generally healthy, though they had the usual childhood illnesses—mumps, measles and German measles and whooping cough. I mind that Frances had the whooping cough very badly. Luckily, neither of them got scarlet fever. Frances had to have her appendix out and Avi had a very severe bout of jaundice in later years.

Decorated doorkies.

Amazingly, they suffered no broken bones. They played outdoors in all weathers and I usually had to call them in for meals and at bedtime, so absorbed were they in their games of rounders, hop-scotch, hide and seek, skipping or plainie/clappie, or in climbing trees, gathering doorkies, or raiding orchards!

They were active at school, too, Frances in particular in athletics and the hockey team, whose exploits are currently being reported in the '44 Years Ago' column in the *Ross-shire Journal*.

We ate as much fish as meat and the children had a teaspoonful of cod liver oil every day, orange juice from the Welfare and school milk. We had poultry only occasionally, usually a chicken during the festive season, or, more rarely still, duck, goose or turkey instead.

The girls were good scholars and usually came away at the end of the school year with some prizes. Frances in particular used to ask me to listen to her chant her Latin (and French and German, too) verbs—'amo, amas, amat …'.

During this time my mother became more and more frail and eventually she gave up her house in Hill Street and she lived with my sister Bess and me turn about. Her mind was as sharp as ever—and that was like a razor!—but her body was breaking down. One day, when she was living with Bess, she slipped on the rug on the polished floor when getting out of bed, and she fell and broke her hip. She never really recovered from this injury and she died on 5 June 1955.

The headstone on my mother and father's grave in Contin churchyard.

She is buried with my father in Contin churchyard. Seldom a day passes that I do not think of her.

Avril took a secretarial course at secondary school (no grants to help you continue your education in her day) and she left school at 16 in 1954 to work in the County Buildings over the railway bridge in Dingwall. In due course she met William Alexander Whyte, who was working in the Commercial Bank (as it was then) in Dingwall. He hailed from Aberfeldy. They married on 18 June 1959 when Bill was 24 and Avi 21. Frances was Avi's bridesmaid and Jimmy Nisbet was Bill's bestman.

At the wedding I fell in love with my husband all over again—he looked so handsome in morning dress!

Avril and Bill lived in Strathpeffer to begin with, but when Bill was shifted to Glasgow in 1960 they moved to Clarkston, where Alan William was born on 1 March 1961. Later that year the family moved to Bishopbriggs, to a new house with space for the youngster to grow up. After trying to have another child without success, they adopted Susan Catherine (b. 15 April 1967), and, as often happens, not long after that Jennifer May was born on 5 November 1969. In 1971 the Whytes then moved to Bridge of Weir, with Bill continuing in (what was by this time) the Royal Bank in Hope Street and later at the Central Branch in Glasgow until his retirement in 1990, while Avril in time resumed work with a timber merchant's at Linwood, close to the airport, where she was office manager until her retirement in 1995.

By the time Frances was in the senior classes of Dingwall Academy, grants were available to enable those who were capable of it to study at university, so she continued her schooling beyond school leaving age, sat and passed her Highers and went on to Glasgow University in 1961. She graduated

The new Mr and Mrs W. A. Whyte at St Clement's Church, Dingwall, 18 June 1959.

The new Mr and Mrs J. R. Hay at the Sherbrooke Hotel, Glasgow, 21 July 1965.

MA in 1964 and did her teacher training year at what was then Jordanhill College of Education in 1965. In her second year at university she met James Roy Hay, who was born in Ayr, and they were married on 21 July 1965—Frances was 22 and Roy, as he is known was 25. Helen Inkson, Frances's school friend, was bridesmaid and Bill Doig, a university friend of Roy's, was bestman.

Roy graduated with a First Class Honours degree in 1965 and he also won the Snell Scholarship. There's a story attached to his taking up the scholarship. John Snell was a seventeenth-century bachelor Ayrshireman who left money in his will for some Glasgow University scholars each year—a classicist and others—to study at Balliol College, Oxford. The scholarship was awarded on the results of an open examination. It was available to unmarried men only, but Roy and Frances were to be married during the time between the award and Roy's taking it up. It so happened that the classicist winner that year was in the same position. At one point it looked as if the two couples would have to 'live in sin', but the terms of Snell's will were varied in the Privy Council to allow them to take up the scholarship as married men. When Christopher Hill, the Master of Balliol, raised the problem with Roy before the change in the terms of the will, the latter said, 'I'm no married yet!'

So Roy took up the scholarship and he and Frances moved to Oxford, where Frances taught in a school in East Oxford where many of the students were the sons of migrants from the subcontinent of India who were employed in the Cowley motor works. Roy duly completed his B.Litt degree from Oxford and the Hays then moved to Norwich, where Roy taught at the University of East Anglia and Frances at the Hewett School. Their first child, Ailsa Margaret, was born there on 6 November 1968. They returned to Glasgow in 1970 and lived in the middle of Glasgow University in Southpark Avenue, where James Ross, who (like his mother and father) is known by his second name, was born on 18 April 1972. Later that year they moved to Lochwinnoch in Renfrewshire.

Jim and I were delighted to have both our daughters in Scotland again and living close to each other, so that they could visit us and each other frequently. But then in 1977 Frances phoned Jim at work (we had no phone at home in those days) to say that Roy had a new job. 'Good,' said Jim. 'Where?' 'In Australia,' she said. There was a long pause and then Jim said, 'Your mother will be devastated'—and so I was! I thought, we will never see the grandchildren again.

They had a big family party (Roy called it a wake!) at 27 Main Street, Lochwinnoch before they emigrated in September 1977. Roy taught in Deakin University in Geelong until his retirement in 2002, while Frances was manager of editorial services there until her retirement in 2000.

With our grandchildren at the back of 27 Main Street, Lochwinnoch, about 1972. Alan at the back, then left to right, Jennifer, Ailsa, Susan and Ross.

Frances, Jim, me and Avril at Frances and Roy's 'wake' in Lochwinnoch before they left for Australia in September, 1977.

MY GRANDCHILDREN AND GREAT-GRANDCHILDREN

Maureen and Alan Whyte, 20 May 1989.

Susan and David Wright, 2 September 1995 (now Fordyce-Wright), with Benjamin.

Jennifer and Alex Scott, 5 December 1997.

Ross and Rebekah Hay, 15 December 2001.

Ailsa Rayner (now divorced) with Dane-Ross and Jessee.

With my Scottish great-grandchildren at the Struie, Ross-shire, October 2003: Ben Fordyce-Wright (standing—13), Frazer Scott (2), Ellie Scott (4), Adam Whyte (7) and Nathan Fordyce-Wright (5).

My Australian great-grandchildren, showing off their gymnastics medals and trophies: Jessee Rayner (7) and Dane-Ross Rayner (10), Cairns, Queensland, 2003.

7

Life's little routines

WE LIVED IN 5 Mansfield for over 39 years and I slaved and cleaned and papered and painted during every one of them! The rooms had very high ceilings, and about the only time Jim and I fell out was over paperhanging. He'd be up the ladder with pasted paper over his shoulder trying to match the pattern and I would say, 'Just a wee bittie over this way', forgetting that he couldn't see the direction in which I was pointing!

I was a full-time wife and mother. In those days, like most people, I had no labour-saving devices—no washing machine or vacuum cleaner. And money was always tight, so we made and mended as much as we possibly could, as most people in our position did. Nobody went hungry and we were all well shod and clothed, but we had to live as economically as possible. For example, Jim would cut out the upper toes of the girls' Clarke's sandals so that they'd get a second year out of them. Jim had a regular wage from his work at Henderson's and he grew virtually all the vegetables and much of the fruit we ate, and mended our shoes. It wasn't a great wage, but Jim handed it all over to me because I managed the money. He propped his unopened pay packet on the mantelpiece every Friday night. I bought his Woodbines for him every day.

I knitted and sewed, always had a Fair Isle jumper and socks on the knitting needles, although my mother was the champion sock knitter—she could turn a heel at the same time as reading her library book! I mended as necessary—turned collars and sheets, patched elbows and darned socks. I baked and cooked, made jam and soup, and cleaned—the black lead grate was a bugbear! Washing was a real chore for we had no hot running water and no bathroom. Eventually we got a gas-fired geyser, and we bathed in a tin bath in front of the fire and I washed the clothes in the sink in the scullery. I starched blouses, dresses and petticoats, and whitened sandshoes—I can see them yet sitting on the windowsill to dry.

Avril, Frances and Richard Whitelock, Jim's sister, Lizzie's son, among the strawberries.

In the garden at 3B Mill Street, in 1984.

The Gardener

Memories are images which came to mind
Some happy, some sad; some the ordinary kind
Jim's garden is one that is a joy to me
He loved it so much, you see.

He planned and he planted vegs, shrubs and flowers
He cosseted the seeds and spent many happy hours
Just looking or hoeing awaiting results
So proud when his marrows confounded his doubts.

Strawberries luscious in their netted beds
Greenhouse tomatoes, rosy and red
Rasps and blackcurrants and goosegogs as well
All seemed to flourish under his spell.

Content in his garden, he said of his toil
That God's hand was aiding him there in the soil.

Jim had his work, of course, but his hobby was gardening. Henderson's allowed him to use part of the field at the top of Mansfield and there he grew all the vegetables we ate (tatties, onions, carrots, turnips, peas, Brussels sprouts, cabbage) and many of the fruits, too (strawberries, raspberries, goosegogs, blackcurrants and redcurrants, apples, pears and plums). Eventually, he got a greenhouse and he grew tomatoes and experimented with all manner of plants, once growing tobacco, which, of course, he could not cure because it was never hot enough for long enough in the North of Scotland. One year Henderson's allowed him to pick the grapes in their greenhouse and he made white wine—it was awful stuff! I made jam with the fruit we did not eat fresh and we wrapped the apples in newspaper and stored them over the winter. Carrots were stored in sacks of sand, potatoes were clamped and we pickled the shallots. That was a job for all the family—lots of tears as we peeled them and the smell of cloves and vinegar lingered for ages!

Jim also spent time on the activities of the Ross-shire Branch of the Seaforth Highlanders' Regimental Association. He was on the executive for 39 years and was secretary for 31 years.

Then there was having visitors and going visiting. My sister Bess and her family lived on the other side of Dingwall and we visited each other turn about once a week on a Thursday afternoon. Ann, Bess's daughter who is ages with Frances, would walk home from school with

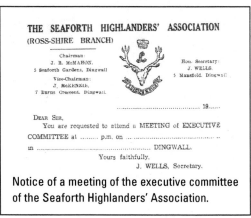

Notice of a meeting of the executive committee of the Seaforth Highlanders' Association.

With my sister, Bess, my much loved twin nieces, Cathie McDonald (left) and Effie Kellow (right), my niece Ann Mackay and nephew Sanders McIntosh at Bess's 90th birthday party in Dingwall in 1997. Sanders visited from Western Australia for the occasion.

Frances when it was Bess's turn to visit me and Frances would come to Bess's house the next week.

My friend of long standing, Peggy Ross, and I also exchanged visits turn about. She lived in Rose Cottage, Maryburgh, so I would go out on the bus to see her, and Jackie, her husband, would drive her in to see me. Margaret, Peggy and Jackie's daughter, who is a teacher in Edinburgh, has kept on the house in Maryburgh and she kindly has me to share New Year's Day dinner with her.

With Peggy and Margaret Ross in 15 Dewar Square, May 1992.

But it wasn't all routine. We hadn't a great deal of spare money for holidays, but we went to Glasgow once when the children were small to visit Jim's sister Lizzie and her family, and in 1952, we hired a bell tent and pitched it in the caravan park at Rosemarkie on the Black Isle. I remember the girls had their first pair of long trousers that year. But even more memorable was the weather, for it was the year of the Lynmouth disaster, when we had very stormy weather all over the country. The River Lyn, which rises on Exmoor and flows into the Bristol Channel, burst its banks and carved a new course through the small town, sweeping all before it. It wasn't as stormy as that in Rosemarkie, but we had heavy rain which the

With Avril and Frances at the caravan at Fortrose in 1953.

Jim, Avril, Frances and the bell tent at Rosemarkie in 1952.

tent could not repel. I remember moving the children around in the night to avoid the drips, and the next day there were heavy seas and the waves crashed over the sea wall.

The next year we hired a caravan at Fortrose, also on the Black Isle. I remember that Frances developed toothache and Jim had to take her back into Dingwall to have a tooth removed. We had forgotten to pack a bread knife—an essential item in those days before sliced bread—and the temporary return to Dingwall allowed us to fetch it from home. We watched the coronation on film in Fortrose village hall.

But a bombshell hit us in 1974 when Henderson's was sold and all the staff were unemployed. Jim had been with the firm for 38 years, so it was a sad time and looking for work was an unwelcome novelty. He wasn't on the dole for long, though, for he soon got a job in Mackay's Garage and Agricultural Company in Tulloch Street as a storeman, which was very like the job he had done latterly in Henderson's, only the goods were different. He was lucky to get a job at 63. It so happened that most of the younger men were chasing the big money at the oilrigs at Nigg at the time.

There were happy events, too, of course. Jim and I celebrated our Golden

Cutting the cake at our Golden Wedding celebration in the Royal Hotel, Dingwall, on 29 December 1983.

Wedding anniversary, one of the happiest days of our lives, with a dinner/dance in the Royal Hotel arranged by our two dearly beloved daughters. Frances visited from Australia for the occasion. The party was held in the Royal Hotel on 29 December 1983, 50 years to the day since our wedding in my parents' house in Contin. Jim was 72 and I was 69. Margaret McKenzie, my bridesmaid, was there but Ian Fraser, Jim's bestman, had died some years before. In his absence my brother Alec spoke about the wedding 50 years before, remarking that he dare not tell any stories about the family at that time in case they ended up 'in one of Cath's famous publications'.

At my 80th birthday party in 1994 with (from left to right) Avril, Bill, Maureen, Jennifer, Alan, Susan and Ben.

With Roy and Frances's ute in Teesdale, Victoria, Australia, March 2002.

8

TRAVELLING AND VISITING

ONCE THE CHILDREN WERE off our hands we had more income at our disposal and we bought a red Hillman Imp. Jim used to drive before the war, but he had to sit for a licence and I learned to drive (in my 50s!) and also got my licence. I was never a very confident driver, though, and after a brush with a motorcyclist (nobody hurt, thank goodness) I gave up driving.

Before that, though, we toured many places locally and had many memorable holidays both in Scotland and abroad. Life was good for us then.

I mind we holidayed in Orkney one year and went to church in Kirkwall on the Sunday, as was our wont. The service was in Gaelic, so we couldn't understand a word of it, but the Minister slipped in a prayer in English, 'for the strangers in our midst'! We hired a caravan one year on the Kintyre Peninsula and loved watching the sun rise over Arran. Another year we went to Trethomas to visit Jock, Jim's brother, and his wife, Joyce. Jim introduced them to each other in 1940, when he was in hospital in Cardiff after he was wounded during the war. We continued that trip by travelling to Oxford to visit Frances and Roy.

I remember a holiday in Spain with Avi and Bill and the children and one in Italy, where we visited Venice.

With the Hillman Imp at Culbokie.

Venice, City of the Waters

Venice, city of the waters
Dreaming all the day
A trembling rainbow jewel
Captured in the sun's ray.

City of the treasures
Cathedral, clock and spire
Vineyards, glass, such beauties
That set the heart afire.

Canals and gondolas
Balconies high above
Tender voices singing
Haunting undying love.

Gliding slowly onwards
Neath the Bridge of Sighs
Oh! City that bewitched me
Eternal never dies.

We also holidayed with Frances and Roy in Australia for three months in 1979/80. I particularly remember Werribee Park between Melbourne and Geelong, where Roy and Frances lived at the time. There was a magnificent mansion house built by two Chirnside brothers, who had made a fortune in wool. I really loved all its features—a very elegant sweeping staircase and panelled rooms, a rose garden, an outdoor zoo, and so on. Frances and Roy hired a camper van and

In Tarra Valley National Park, Gippsland, Victoria, 1980.

we toured Gippsland, the part of the state Victoria lying east of Melbourne, the children and their parents sleeping under canvas, and Jim and I in the van. We zig-zagged between the Great Dividing Range and the coast, day about, so we experienced a wide range of environments. One day we travelled north beside the Snowy River to Buchan, where there are magnificent limestone caves with stalagmites and stalactites, and on past Seldom Seen Filling Station (Frances said, 'I've seen it', to which Roy replied, 'You've only seen it once!') to McKillop's Bridge over the river.

Australia So Fair

In that far away land that's Australia
Where the bright sun shines each day
Where the surf beats the shore on 'The Great Ocean Way'
And the scent of the gum trees holds sway
Jacarandas and hibiscus are all colour lent
To the beautiful country Australia.

Mountains and rivers, deserts and creeks
Birds of bright feathers on dense mountain peaks
Kangaroos bounding, opossums and snakes
Emus so stately, black swans on the lakes
Bridges o'er rivers, marvels in wood
McKillop's I mention where once I stood
And looked down o'er the 'Snowy' and marvelled anew
How vast is this country Australia.

Scallop boats at 'Lakes Entrance'
Buchan's limestone caves
Port Campbell with trees for the soldiers so brave
'Twelve Golden Apostles' guarding the waves
Of this land that's Australia.

Magnificent cities, gold fields of old
Sheep by the million that is wealth untold,
Great Captain Cook the explorer so bold
Who discovered this land that's Australia.

Cairns with gardens under the sea
And Ayers Rock that great mystery
A museum of shells a wonder to see
Flamingos in pink tutus, an elegance of grace
Waterfalls that cascade lacy, frothy in space
Iron-laced houses of Victorian days
And Werribee is one to amaze
Darwin's philosophy a topic to debate
Fairy Penguins and King Emperors all go to make
That wonderful land, Australia so fair.

We also had a memorable holiday in Ayrshire when Frances and Roy were on holiday from Australia in 1982, during the Falklands War. Roy's parents arranged for the extended Hay and Wells families to holiday in the stables at Blairquhan estate, in Straiton, where Roy spent much of his childhood. There were 22 of us, with three dogs and a cat, and we had some memorable picnics and dinner parties which always ended with games and singing. Roy maintained that Maggie Thatcher didn't face the logistic problems we did when trying to organise everybody to go anywhere. The younger members of the family looked after the meals, but one night they phoned in a massive order for a Chinese carryout from Ayr, the nearest town. When they went to pick it up, they discovered that the restaurant hadn't even begun the meals because they were convinced, by the size of the order, that it had been a hoax!

I visited Australia again in 2002 with Pat and Ian Morrison. Pat is the sister of my son-in-law Roy, and she is married to Ian Morrison, the Inverness solicitor who hails from Beauly. For some years now, since travelling to Avril's family became out of the question for me during the winter, Pat and Ian have kindly invited me to their house for Christmas dinner, and they accompanied me on the journey to and from Frances and Roy's new home in the country at Teesdale near Geelong and about 80 miles from Melbourne. I kept a diary of that holiday and here are some extracts from it:

Saturday March 2nd.
After breakfast we started off in convoy, Pat and Ian in their hired car, Roy leading the way via Shelford, Rokewood and Skipton where we stopped for coffee at the roadhouse. Thence along the Glenelg Highway (Aussie name for our main road) to Streatham, and then on to Rossbridge (couldn't resist a photo!) and Mafeking.

Most of the time I felt quite at home as the names and locations had such a Scottish flavour which was quite heart-warming, but the wide open spaces really were amazing and the miles and miles of sky seemed to go on for ever and ever. The gum trees were with us, marching along, sometimes in small groups, or perhaps a solitary one stark against the sky. They were very curious to me as their formation is not symmetrical as most of our trees are. You can pin point a fir, an oak or, my favourite, the dainty silver birch, but the gum trees have foliage quite dense lower down and then seem to sprout in all directions, topped with an umbrella shape of branches—very, very distinctive, once seen never forgotten. There are 200 varieties and all flower. As it was Australia's autumn, most flowering was over. They shed their bark as well as their leaves and then become very untidy looking.

We seemed to have been travelling a long way and yet the Grampian Mountains, our destination, seemed no nearer. Actually the distance from Teesdale, our home base, was 200 miles. But we pressed on. The roads were very good. Now and again we came to a stretch of dirt road which the Aussies call 'washboard roads', but I could never remember this and called them 'corduroy roads'. There are no passing places as we know them, but they have a tacit agreement that, on meeting an oncoming vehicle on a narrow road, you put 'one wheel on the dirt', that is what we would call the hard shoulder.

We reached the Grampians near Mt William, which is about the middle of the steep range stretching from Mt Abrupt near Dunkeld in the south to Mt Zero in the north. I could not remember the Mt Abrupt name, so I renamed it Mount Hiccup and that it will always be to me!

The galahs with their pink and grey feathers appeared and disappeared. It became less remote as more and more buildings came into sight. Lake Bellfield was passed by before we arrived at the Grampian Motel. The owner, Peter Bongiorno, used to work in Geelong, accommodating overseas students for Deakin University. When the bookings were made, he had asked Roy to bring a *Geelong Advertiser*, the local paper.

There were lots of kangaroos around. They were very tame, but we were advised not to pat them because they were verminous. We had three adjoining rooms at the back, very quiet with a great view. Dumping our luggage, we set off for Halls Gap which was seething with tourists, every conceivable nationality in looks and dress. Every piece of vacant ground in between the trees was taken up with tents and caravans. All seemed in carnival mood. Lunch was at one of the cafes situated in a little glen where the magpies flittered around waiting for titbits, just like the Dingwall gulls. Not wasting any time, we drove up a very twisting road to the Silverband turntable, a lookout with views down over the valley to the mountains beyond. It was steep in parts, but I managed it with help.

The Grampians are a very long range of mountains, not very high, none as high as our very own Ben Wyvis, more for walkers than climbers. They seemed to go on forever, and no matter how often you looked they seemed to show a different aspect every time. I sent several postcards back home. The very name, and also the McKenzie Falls, was so Scottish, as are many of the creeks, such as Reid, Sutherland, Henderson etc. Reminded me of home at every turn. I did not even attempt to use my camera. One simply could not do them justice.

Back down to the village. We just managed to get into the Aboriginal Centre at Brambuk before closing time. We bought postcards and fridge magnets. Frances bought me a lovely scarf, while Pat and Ian availed themselves of the souvenirs on show. It was all so very interesting. Aborigines believe that if anything is made or built in a straight way, it is bad luck and so, to confuse their evil spirits, everything is crooked, even the archway into the Centre is crooked—off centre.

Back again to the motel for a wash, brush and change of clothing to have dinner at the Tavern. The menu was varied and strange. There was emu and kangaroo, and a tropical fish called barramundi.

And so to bed and I slept like a top!

We all met up in the morning for breakfast in the motel dining room. Soon we were on our way again via Halls Gap up the Zumsteins Road to the McKenzie Falls. Roy thought the way in to the falls would be too rough for me but there was another shorter way to a fine look out, well protected by very strong iron fencing. It was fantastic and as I looked upwards to the higher lookout I was really glad I did not attempt it. From where I was the higher lookout seemed to be jutting out far across the falls.

At the McKenzie Falls in the Victorian Grampians, 2002.

• • •

Frances shops at Bannockburn, a small town between Teesdale and Geelong in which there is a sizeable supermarket. Its size is puzzling until you realise that the countryside round about is more densely populated than it seems from the road. The giveaway is the letterboxes at the road ends. There were all kinds of letterboxes, but the most common was a kerosene tin on its side minus its lid, with a name in white paint. I thought the absolute ultimate was the letterbox deluxe—a defunct (I presume) *microwave oven!* That was one snap I made sure of for the album!

An unusual letterbox!

9

THESE THINGS ARE SENT TO TRY US

JIM RESIGNED FROM HIS job with Mackay's before we went for three months' holiday with Frances and Roy in Australia in 1979/80. He also resigned as secretary of the Ross-shire Branch of the Seaforth Highlanders' Regimental Association at their 32nd annual reunion dinner, a position he had held for 31 years. He became sick towards the end of our holiday in Australia, and he visited the doctor and took to his bed for a few days, a very rare event. With hindsight, I wonder if he knew in his own mind about the illness that eventually killed him before we left for Australia and if that was his reason for

Jim in 1985.

resigning from Mackay's and from the Seaforths (and for making the journey to Australia, for that matter). At any rate, he was still not fully well for the journey home to Scotland, so it was a bit of a nightmare. However, in time he recovered and returned to work part time at Mackay's, who were eager to have him back again. He liked the structure regular work gave to his day.

But we were not so happy at 5 Mansfield and went house hunting again. We had been in Mansfield for over 39 years, which is a long time to accumulate a lot of rubbish, so we had to get rid of loads of stuff. We decided not to look for an old folks house because Jim still enjoyed his gardening and there's not much scope for that in sheltered accommodation. Then 3B Mill Street fell vacant and we flitted in 1984. It turned out to be a cold house, with the toilet, bathroom and bedrooms upstairs, and we were only two years there when Jim became ill and the garden and stairs became a liability.

Jim's headstone in Mitchell Hill Cemetery, Dingwall.

Eventually, prostate cancer was diagnosed. Jim had two operations to relieve the symptoms, but they were stopgap measures only and no chemotherapy or radiotherapy was suggested. It was my privilege to look after him myself at home. But I cannot describe to you how soul-destroying it is to watch the person you love above all others, and have spent 52 years of married life with, deteriorate day by day, knowing that there is nothing you can do to alter the eventual end, which came for Jim on the morning of 24 October 1985, when he died in his own bed in his own home.

At his funeral service the minister captured him well when he said in his eulogy:

'… I believe that this old soldier might have preferred to fade away without too much stir and public observance … he had a decisive and firm way of thinking: his yea was yea and his nay a clear nay …'

I was never really happy in Mill Street. Frances stayed on a while with me after the funeral and before she left she got an application form from the Council for an old folks house, which I completed and signed. She personally went to the County Buildings and delivered it. Some time passed and I hadn't received any word whatsoever. I went myself and was told that no such document was found in their files. Strange! I was furious and really let them know that. So when the house I am in now, 15 Dewar Square, came up, I haunted them night and day. Eventually, in 1986, I got tenancy, next door to Mrs Frances Inkson. I have been here for 18 years and I do like it.

I was lonely without Jim, so when I moved to Dewar Square I decided to get a cat for company. I always liked cats and we seldom were without one, from Tarzan when I was first married, to Smokey whom we had in Mansfield and then to Tobee, who became my beloved companion in

Frances Inkson, my neighbour in Dewar Square, and her daughter Helen, who was Frances's bridesmaid.

Tobee, October 1989.

Dewar Square. When I first got him from the vet he could sit in the palm of my hand. The mother had either been killed or had abandoned him. The vet gave me a baby's bottle to feed him with. I was sure he would not survive, but eventually he graduated to milk off a spoon and then to Heinz baby food, just like a baby. I called him Tobee because when I first got him I wasn't sure whether he was a he or a she, and, I just said to my friend, 'Tobee or not to be', and the name stuck. He followed me everywhere, even when I went round the doors for the poppy collection. He brought pleasure to my neighbour, too, whose own cat had died, going to her house every morning for his (second) breakfast. I used to tuck messages in his collar and send him next door. I used to say he was the 'cat express' rather than the 'pony express'.

One day, when he was 10 years old, Tobee did not return home. We searched everywhere for him but to no avail, then a week later his body was found in an old broken-down shed in a garden nearby which he had obviously crawled into to die. There wasn't a mark on him and I think he had eaten weedkiller or slug

With my daughters on one of Frances's visits from Australia in 1991.

bait from somebody's garden. He is now buried in my garden wrapped in an oval-shaped rug which was made by the mother of Mrs Matheson, who was the landlady of Aultguish Inn where I had my first job at the age of 14. My daughter Frances used to urge me to get another cat, but I could not bear the agony if anything happened to one, so I will not.

I was delighted when Avi and Bill decided to move back to Dingwall in 1997 when Avril retired for her position as office manager with the timber company in Linwood, where she had worked for many years. They bought a flat in the old distillery buildings and I was so pleased to have them near and be able to see a lot more of them. I loved the period when they lived there.

But disaster struck again in late 1998 when Avi was diagnosed with inoperable bowel cancer and she and Bill returned south to be nearer their children and the specialist hospital where she underwent extensive chemotherapy and radiotherapy. At first she wondered if there had been a mistake because she felt so well, and she and Bill went on holiday cruising down the Rhine on a barge. She tolerated the chemotherapy very well, too, but the radiotherapy made her very sick and she lost all her hair, which distressed her greatly. Frances came home to see her in June 2001 and we had a party for my 87th birthday at which Avi looked better than she had done for a while.

Avi gradually became more ill, however, and began to suffer dizzy spells,

With my daughters at my 87th birthday party in Largs, in 2001.

With Belle (middle), Bess (right) at Donnie and Eileen's (Bess's son) Golden Wedding celebration on 20 March 1989. Avril used to call us the 'Andrew's Sisters' because we liked to sing together on such occasions.

which were caused by a tumour in her head. The operation to remove it went well, but she never really recovered after that and she died on 10 October 2001, almost three years since she was diagnosed. I was privileged to be with her, along with all her family, and she was at peace.

I worried constantly, and impotently, about her every day of her illness. I found it so difficult to talk to her about it, for she invariably said she was 'fine' when you asked how she was. Her answer was an attempt to shield the person she was talking to and she never complained. Her son Alan bravely spoke about his mother at her funeral service and stressed that she liked to be in control, and the song 'My Way' was played at her request. These two comments were so true of her. I so admired her independent spirit and think of her every day. The order of her passing is against nature—you don't expect your children to die before you do.

You can't give up, though, and so life goes on, and though I dearly miss my husband still and my elder daughter, I am blessed and privileged to be here and able to write this story in my 90th year.

I am as happy as can be expected and pleased to be able to live in my own home and be as independent as possible. I am very deaf, have recently had cataracts removed from both eyes and suffer from angina, but otherwise I feel quite well—with the help of the many pills my doctors gives me! I have a home help and can no longer mow the grass or cut the hedge, but I still wash my own clothes, cook my own meals (even still make jam with the raspberries growing in the back garden), and plant annuals and bulbs in the front garden, according to the seasons.

I get about, too, though often by taxi now—shopping, to church and the coffee mornings, to the library and to the many activities arranged for senior citizens in Dingwall. I must admit, though, that as you get older and there are fewer and fewer of your contemporaries left, social occasions can be trying events. You remember so clearly those who are no longer with you—my beloved Jim and my daughter Avril, my mother and father, all my siblings and Billy and Alex, my friends Peggy Ross and Frances Inkson, and former neighbours and friends.

But my remaining relatives visit as often as they can—Bill, my son-in-law in Houston, and his and Avril's children and their children; even Frances and her husband Roy visit quite frequently from Australia as Ross, their son, and Rebekah, his wife, did when they were living in Scotland, though it is many years since I saw Ailsa, their daughter, and I have never met my Australian great-grandchildren. And I am blessed with good neighbours and very attentive nieces who live locally, especially Cathie McDonald (who has her own troubles), Effie Kellow and Margaret McKenzie.

And I have my memories!

10

REFLECTIONS OF A WRITER

I WAS ALWAYS AN avid reader and penned poems and stories as far back as I can remember. At school, I liked writing stories, sometimes about an imaginative world of my own. The only books we had in house when I was a child were the Bible, *Pilgrim's Progress*, a *Chambers Journal* and a copy of the Brahan Seer's predictions. Much later we took the *People's Journal* and my mother liked the *My Weekly*. I like words and enjoy doing crossword puzzles, and, if I have nothing to read, I will happily take up the dictionary and explore some of the words there.

I enjoy reading fiction and books about travel. I especially like novels by Wilbur Smith, the South African author, whose books are usually about the gold mines in that country. The local library is a gold mine for me.

Ode to the Library Ladies

It's a pleasure to visit the library
The ladies there are so kind
So many helpful suggestions
About how to broaden the mind.

And if you are forgetful
Indeed, it's common to all
Your bookmark that has gone missing
Is pinned up there on the wall.

In fact it makes me consider
As I view the odd dozen there
How the people who left them behind
Don't seem to bother or care.

Serenely you answer our questions
And if the print is too small
You'll look up all the quotations
And it's no bother at all.

So many sections to browse through
We could easily spend all of the day
Then discovering our time is limited
We regretfully choose, and away.

Tables and chairs for our comfort
Tall windows to let in the light
The atmosphere ever so restful
The decor cheerful and bright.

Though we plague you with titles
About this book or that
You promptly write out a ticket
And soon it comes out of a hat.

Then via a voice on the phone
Just a message to say
If you like to visit the library
That book has come in today.

People do well to remember
That all this reading is free
Given by the Scots benefactor
The courtesy of Andrew Carnegie.

Good luck to the library ladies
May you always be there
To brighten and cheer up our visits
With all your courtesy and care.

But I also enjoy rereading the classics. I found a copy of R. M. Ballantine's *Coral Island* just the other day.

Ink in the Blood

When the time has come
And life runs out
The pen is still forever
No more lines to set in rhyme
No more tales on paper
All my life has been
An affair with words
A fascinating journey
Always new, never boring
With a dictionary for company

A word, a thought, an idea
With a heavenly direction
Goes gaily on like a rushing river
Gold that is never bought
Spontaneous words
That come unbidden
Like seed on the ground.

I'm sure my pen is mightier than a sword as it feels quite heavy today.

In my 90th year.